CARING FOR THE
self

CARING FOR THE
soul

A Book
of Spiritual
Development

PHILIP ST. ROMAIN

LIGUORI/TRIUMPH
LIGUORI, MISSOURI

Published by Liguori/Triumph
An Imprint of Liguori Publications
Liguori, Missouri
http://www.liguori.org

Library of Congress Cataloging-in-Publication Data

St. Romain, Philip A.
    Caring for the self, caring for the soul : a book of spiritual direction / Philip St. Romain.—1st ed.
        p. cm.
    ISBN 0-7648-0593-2 (pbk.)
    1. Spirituality—Catholic Church. I. Title.

BX2350.65 .S72 2000
248.4'82—dc21   99-086477

Parts of this work previously appeared in *The Handbook of Spiritual Growth* and *The "Logic" of Happiness*, both published by Liguori Publications, Liguori, Missouri.

Printed in the United States of America
04 03 02 01 00   5 4 3 2 1
First Edition

CARING FOR THE
self

CARING FOR THE
soul

CONTENTS

INTRODUCTION IX

1 THE ESSENCE OF CHRISTIAN SPIRITUALITY 1

What Is Spirituality? 2
Consciousness and Spirituality 5
Three Types of Christian Spirituality 6
The "Work" of Christian Spirituality 8
True Spirituality and the Cross 9

2 GOD, SELF, AND THE SOUL 11

"I" to "I" 12
"I" Owns the Functions 12
God Is; I Am; We Are 13
The Seeing "I" 14
I Am 15
Christian Enlightenment 16
The Coming of Enlightenment 17
Christ: God's Self-Image 18
About God 19
That-I-Am 20
The Nature of the Soul 21
Happiness and the True Self 25

The "Way" to Happiness 27
Reality, Sanity, and Wisdom 28
Destiny and Control 30
Spiritual Growth 31

3 SPIRITUALITY AND THE HUMAN CONDITION 33

The Ego and the Unconscious Self 35
Human Brokenness: How We Lose Contact
    With God 36
The False Self: Sickness of Soul 38
Characteristics of the False Self System 43
Inventory of Inordinate Desires and Delusions 45
Addictive Behaviors Checklist 47
A Litany of Hope for a Sick Soul 48
Changing Your Behavior 49

4 CENTERING YOUR LIFE IN GOD'S CARE 51

Discovering Your Images of God 52
Belonging to God 53
Walking With Christ 55
A Prayerful Celebration
    of Entrusting and Commitment 56
The Holy Spirit 58
The Gifts of the Holy Spirit 59
The Eucharist 61
The Basics of Personal Prayer 62
True Prayer 65
Spiritual Direction:
    Companion on the Spiritual Journey 66
How Spiritual Direction Works 68
On Making a Retreat 71

5 RECONCILIATION AND INNER
TRANSFORMATION 76

Renewal of Mind 78
Examen of Current Relationships 79
Preparing for Reconciliation With Others 80
Reconciling With Others 82
Daily Examen 85
The Sacrament of Reconciliation 87

6 LIVING IN THE SPIRIT 88

Meeting Your True Needs 90
Sharing Your Giftedness 92
Discerning God's Will 93
Guidelines for Healthy Relationships 96
Carrying Your Crosses 98
Rhythm for Daily Living 100
Tracking the Spiritual Journey 102

7 HOW TO *BE* A MYSTIC 109

Anthropology 110
Enlightenment 113
Christology 116
Mystical Theology 117
Affirmations for Realizing the True Self 118

8 EXERCISES FOR BREAKING FREE 120

How to Disturb Yourself Most of the Time:
    An Awareness Exercise 121
Attitude Check 122
Affirmations for a Loving Attitude 123
An Exercise for Inner Healing 127
The Nature of Attachments 129
The Serenity Prayer: A Meditation 132
Dynamics of the Heart 134
Guidelines for Christian Prayer 136
Characteristics of Detachment 138

9 NUGGETS FROM THE STREAM OF LIFE 139

Proverbs and Practical Wisdom
    for Spiritual Living 139

SUGGESTED READING 147

INTRODUCTION

We are a spiritual people.

The truth of this statement may be discovered by reflecting on the experience of being human.

Is it not true that we yearn for fulfillment, for an answer to the question "What is life all about?" Doesn't there seem to be within us a certain emptiness, a certain hunger, that cannot be easily filled?

Such questions, and others that flow from deep within us in moments of reflection, meditation, or sometimes even just exhaustion, are reflective of a core spiritual nature within the human person. The search for answers to these questions leads us on what might be understood as a journey. When we put the two experiences together, we discover that each of us is a spiritual person on a journey of spiritual development.

My own experiences of being on a journey of spiritual growth have led me to conclude that, for whatever reason, we are created in this way or—if not created—we became this way through choice and decision. It may not have always been through our own personal choices and decisions but possibly through a corporate, original choice and decision. (See Genesis 3:1–19.) This journeying, questioning self seems to have something to do with who we are.

If you find yourself in some agreement with the experiences described, if you have discovered yourself faced with the experience of "needing to be filled," then you may also resonate with the experience of trying all sorts of different paths seeking to be filled.

Each of us grows spiritually in different ways. We make a series of choices and decisions, believing that somehow we may discover something or someone that will fill us. This pattern, this experience, is nothing to be ashamed of, nothing to run from or deny. It seems to be pretty normal to the human experience.

The first place we usually turn to be filled is to the material world. We assume that the hunger within us is a hunger that can be filled with "stuff," and so we begin the process of accumulating.

At first, accumulation does seem to satisfy us. However, as time goes on we discover that the stuff of life just doesn't seem to do it for us. There doesn't seem to be enough stuff—enough money, enough relationships—to fill us and make us whole. In a moment of honesty, we might admit that all we have succeeded in doing is to distract ourselves, to take a detour on our path to spiritual growth. But we haven't begun to deal with the real issue at hand.

It is only after this initial experience, this false start, if you will, that we are really able to begin. It is at this point that you will find *Caring for the Self, Caring for the Soul* to be useful and important. When you begin a spiritual quest, it is important to have a map or a guide or someone who can lead you and point you in the right direction. A good guide is essential. It is hoped that this book will serve as a map to get you on track in this journey.

You can use this book in a number of ways. For example, you can go through it by yourself to deepen your own spiritual growth; this is probably the way most people use it. If you have a spiritual director or companion that you meet with on occasion, you might share some of your work with him or her; you might want to make specific references to the book and ask for suggestions on which exercises you need to be working at this time. This book would also be a valuable resource for faith-sharing groups to use; some of the exercises work well in this context. Religious education teachers will find here a variety of aids on the topic of spirituality.

Some of the resources made available in this book were initially published in two separate volumes: *Handbook for Spiritual Growth* and *The "Logic" of Happiness*. The *Handbook* was a fairly straightforward collection of materials I had developed through the years for certain retreats, and the exercises were developed to use with people in spiritual direction. *"Logic"* featured selections of a much more personal and intuitive nature. Both books "had their day" and served their purpose.

In many ways, it now seems that these two books were complementary works. The *Handbook* described something of the objective disciplines of the spiritual life, while *"Logic"* related my own experiences, insights, and struggles on the spiritual journey. Bringing them together in this new work, *Caring for the Self, Caring for the Soul,* makes for a more complete collection of both practical and inspirational resources.

Whatever your need, I hope you will find something helpful in this work to encourage and support you in your spiritual growth. Enjoy your journey.

1

THE ESSENCE
OF CHRISTIAN
SPIRITUALITY

———

Cling to nothing. Consciousness unfolds in stages and in ways you cannot
even predict. There are times for
thinking, times for studying, times for
being sensately present, times for
creativity, times for feeling, times for
being lost in emptiness. It is all important. Let it happen as it will. Follow
your heart. Don't force anything.

christian spirituality is a topic about which
volumes have been written by many different authors. Any
single aspect of Christian spirituality, such as its history or its
various modes of expression, could involve hundreds of pages
of reflection and documentation.

However, I am presenting here a brief sketch of what I call the essence of Christian spirituality. In using the term *essence*, I refer to what is at the heart of all the various forms of Christian spirituality—monastic, clerical, religious, lay, and other. Although these various spiritualities embody different lifestyles, they all do so out of a common center of faith and concern. Once we grasp this center, we can easily see how Christian spirituality differs from other non-Christian spiritualities. We can also begin to discern our own individual and unique manner of expressing the spiritual life.

WHAT IS SPIRITUALITY?

To understand what spirituality is, let us compare it with two similar but not identical concerns: religion and morality. *Religion* is a *living tradition of wisdom and worship*. In this context, "living" refers to a group of people who practice this "religion." It is not something merely found in a book; rather, it is a community of believers. "Tradition" refers to a body of truth passed on within a community of believers, from one generation to the next, through written and other means. "Wisdom" describes those teachings that point out the relationship between the community of believing human beings and the Divine and how to live out this relationship. Finally, "worship" refers to the rituals and other means the community of believers uses to celebrate the relationship with the Divine, both individually and communally.

Morality is the *practice of behavioral principles* for conduct that furthers the *common good*. "Practice," as used here, refers to a repeated effort to do something, and "behavioral principles" are those values that encourage certain behaviors while discouraging others. The "common good" is the goal toward which moral behavior tends, which, of course, can be defined in many different ways.

Compared to "religion" and "morality," we now look at *spirituality*—emphasizing Christian spirituality in particular. Spirituality is *a way of life* that ensues from a particular *center of meaning and value*, bringing a particular quality of *energy* and *awareness* to the one who follows this way of life.

A way of life is the manner in which one actually lives one's lifestyle. In particular, Christian spirituality aims to take seriously Jesus' call to follow him. Christian spirituality is one's individual efforts to make the life of Christ visible in his or her unique situation.

Center of meaning and value refers to that which one lives for, that which is of most importance or of ultimate concern. In Christian spirituality, this center of meaning and value is focused in Jesus Christ, who is the giver of the indwelling Spirit and who is the way to the transcendent Father. Hence, Christian spirituality is a Trinitarian spirituality; Jesus is not to be worshiped to the exclusion of the Father and the Spirit. To overemphasize or underemphasize devotion to any of the Persons of the Trinity would be to lose the kind of centeredness that Christian spirituality invites.

Energy is the quality of aliveness in an individual's life, the power to do something. Love for God, the human community and, indeed, all of creation is the energy that characterizes the Christian. This love moves in the direction of creating a human community that images the love of the Trinity and a planetary harmony that images the harmony and peace of heaven.

Finally, *awareness* pertains to one's alertness and perception, how one sees things, what is seen, and "who" sees. Christian spirituality sees the whole of creation as the work of God. Consequently, Christian spirituality does not reject the world as illusory or human affairs as an obstacle to spiritual growth. Rather, Christian spirituality is alert to the goodness of God revealed in the human heart, in creation, and in all of history.

In other words, Christian spirituality is interested in the events of the day.

With this understanding of religion, morality, and spirituality, what relationships might we find among the three?

1. *It is possible to be moral without being especially religious or spiritual.* Such might be the case with an agnostic humanist, who works for the common good but not from any particular religious tradition and without firm allegiance to any particular center of meaning and value.
2. *It is possible to be religious without being spiritual or moral.* Such religiosity characterized many of the scribes and the Pharisees of Jesus' time. In such cases, which continue to abound in this age, one could be familiar with the tradition and participate in its rituals but not be committed to living out a particular center of meaning and value. In fact, attachment to religious dogmas and rituals could be an obstacle to spirituality for some.
3. *It is possible to live spiritually without being committed to any particular religion.* Many people are doing so in this day. They generally believe in a good and loving God but pledge no allegiance to any particular religion and worship with no community. Frequently, they are eclectic in their beliefs about God, picking and choosing from various religions. They are living a spirituality, however, in that they honestly try to center their lives and motives in these truths.
4. *It is impossible to live a spiritual life without living a moral life.* Any authentic center of meaning and value ought to encourage behavior to benefit the common good. Hence, spirituality is of a higher level of concern than morality, and morality is foundational to spirituality.

5. *Although one can be spiritual without being religious, it is far better if a spirituality is informed by a religious body of truth, supported by a community of believers, and celebrated ritually.* Without religion, spirituality can easily lose its focus and become too eclectic, too ecumenical, and too soft-headed.

6. *Ideally, religion ought to be the means by which people embrace the moral life and enter into the spiritual journey.* Religion issues *the* invitation to the moral and spiritual life and provides the tools, wisdom, and support for living this life.

> *B*eing preoccupied and living in a fog
> of desires, unresolved emotional pain,
> intellectual confusion, a state of being
> asleep to ourselves and life: This is how
> most people live! How sad! How to
> wake them up?

CONSCIOUSNESS AND SPIRITUALITY

Consciousness pertains to states of awareness, and there are many to be experienced along the way. Physiology, diet, and temperament have a profound effect on one's state of consciousness—so do personal judgments about what is happening.

It is easy to get caught in the trap that *more* consciousness means that one is somehow *more* spiritual. But spirituality pertains to the *quality* of consciousness, not to its quantity. Is consciousness peaceful, open to life, willing to share? Or is it self-focused, closed, irritable, fearful?

Growth in consciousness enables a more mature spirituality. The more awareness and energy, the more there is to share. But growth in consciousness does not guarantee love. It seems to me that the converse is true, however, especially if one comes to suffer for the sake of love. Then will consciousness be filled with compassion.

> *A ccept whatever state of consciousness you are experiencing now in gratitude. Do not say, "I should be experiencing my life another way!" This is self-rejection, the cause of division.*

THREE TYPES OF CHRISTIAN SPIRITUALITY

All Christian spiritualities have in common the characteristics listed in the previous pages. Nevertheless, there are three general "ways of life" that attempt to express the meaning of Christ. Each way of life has a long and rich history and are especially designed to serve the needs of people living out of an apostolic spirituality. The following describe these three "ways of life."

Monastic spirituality

- *Examples:* Carthusians, Trappists, Benedictines, Cistercians
- *Style of life:* Regular, simple, ascetical, familial
- *Tonality:* Flight from the world
- *Involvement with the world:* Little; only with those who come to them
- *Organization:* Hierarchical-familial

- *Apostolate:* One of testimony; a witness of faith
- *Prayer:* Divine Office; Prayer of the Hours

Psychological-contemplative spirituality

- *Examples:* Carmelites, Poor Clares, Dominicans, Passionists, Charismatics
- *Style of life:* Regular, familial, not as simple and ascetical as monastic
- *Tonality:* "We have not here a lasting city."
- *Involvement with the world:* Very limited
- *Organization:* Familial-hierarchical
- Apostolate: More involved with people than the monastic but primarily through the ministry of prayer
- *Prayer:* Liturgy of the Hours; private contemplation

Apostolic spirituality

- *Examples:* Laypeople, diocesan priests, Redemp–torists, Jesuits, many religious orders
- *Style of life:* Irregular; complex; not as ascetical/familial
- *Tonality:* Incarnational
- *Involvement with the world:* Very much "in" the world, but not "of" the world
- *Organization:* Discerning-professional; many different kinds of organizational patterns
- *Apostolate:* Direct; involved; incarnational; transforming the world into the kingdom of God
- *Prayer:* Not much emphasis on Liturgy of the Hours, more on private prayer/contemplation, self-knowledge, "finding God in all things," prayer encompassing daily living

*H*abits of thought, speech, and
attention concentrate energy in different
parts of the body. These are uncoiled
and heard as the Spirit cleanses the
soul. Let it happen. Enjoy it.

THE "WORK" OF CHRISTIAN SPIRITUALITY

In order to live a life imaging the love of Christ, we must transform everything within ourselves that moves in a contrary direction. This calls for hard work, perseverance, and plenty of prayer. The hard work might be summarized under the following goals, each of which will be developed more fully in the chapters to come.

- *Letting go of disordered desires and attachments:* If our heart and its desires are centered on worldly and unspiritual concerns, then we need to see this clearly and establish new priorities. The False Self in each of us is the source of our disordered desires. "For where your treasure is, there your heart will be also" (Lk 12:34).
- *Centering our lives in God through Christ:* As spiritually centered persons, we love God above all and seek to have our will conformed to the will of God. In giving up disordered attachments, it becomes possible to begin growing in faith. "You shall love the LORD your God with all your heart, and with all your soul, and with all your might" (Deut 6:5).
- *Healing and reconciliation:* We must let go of all resentment, shame, and anxious preoccupation, for

these keep us bound to the past and allow the False Self to make a claim on the will. "...and forgive us our debts, as we also have forgiven our debtors" (Mt 6:12).

- *Changing old attitudes*: If we are to remain free from negative emotions and peaceful in the present moment, we must change the way we think about ourselves, other people, creation, and God's will. "Do not be conformed to this world, but be transformed by the renewing of your minds, so that you may discern what is the will of God—what is good and acceptable and perfect" (Rom 12:2).

- *Living daily*: We learn to live one day at a time, doing each day what must be done, learning from the past, hoping in the future. We also learn to meet our own needs in a new way, without the complications of the False Self. "So do not worry about tomorrow, for tomorrow will bring worries of its own. Today's trouble is enough for today" (Mt 6:34).

The kind of spiritual practice you undertake determines the kind of person you will become. This practice, in turn, is informed by your vision of life. Do not scorn good teaching. It has its place.

TRUE SPIRITUALITY AND THE CROSS

The obstacles to spiritual growth are selfishness, preoccupation, anxiety, and various forms of material and psychological idolatry.

When we are centered in love and willing to love, the energies of the False Self and its disordered desires confront us daily.

The spiritual journey is fun as long as it is easy. But when love calls for us to hang in there or to do something we do not want to do—even hate to do—then there is a civil war within. The cross is the suffering we must endure to remain true to Love, the confrontation of our own inner hostility and selfishness. It is the encounter with our internalization of a sick, sick world.

Through carrying this cross, we lose our attraction to sin and we become transformed—raised up, as it were—in Love.

And true spirituality is Love.

What is the inner resistance to loving without reserve?

Sin!

What is its root?

The fearful, False Self!

How to get rid of the False Self?

The cross: Love that endures even in the face of pain.

2

GOD, SELF,
AND THE SOUL

————

If you desire true happiness, then
spirituality will bring you there. If you
seek more—wealth, power, recognition, being "special"—then spirituality will not be enough. Neither will
anything else!

for those of us who begin to seriously pursue a
more spiritual life, questions pertaining to who God is, what
we are, and how we are connected with God are sure to arise.
As we look to the world religions for answers, we find a wide
variety of responses. At one extreme is the position that human
individuality, or an individual self, is naught but an illusion
created by the mind; only God, or Ultimate Reality, is real.
Contrasting this pantheism is an extreme dualism which asserts
that God and creation are so radically distinct and opposed
that God has little involvement in creation, leaving it pretty

much to fend for itself. Interestingly, both of these extreme positions can be found in most world religions.

In this section, I share a variety of reflections and observations on God, Self, and Soul. Some of these come from personal experiences and insights; others come from what mystics and theologians have written. There are no final answers here, of course—only pointers, at best.

"I" TO "I"

For me, the human "I" is the observer-in-freedom; the "I" sees (awareness) and chooses the direction of its seeing (freedom). A state of consciousness, then, can be viewed as an energetic medium in which the "I" experiences and exercises itself. The "I" sees and moves in and out of psychosomatic states; it transcends these states while being immanent within them. For the unenlightened, states of consciousness might be considered experiences of the "I" but this is delusion and attachment of "I-to-states." "I" is "that" which moves in and out of states of consciousness. "I" does not create itself; it simply "is." The "I" receives its existence, in each moment, from the hand of the One who gives life and form.

Every person is a Self-becoming. If you know this for yourself, you will see it in others.

"I" OWNS THE FUNCTIONS

The senses are for being in the here and now, in loving silence.

The intellect is a talking computer, storing information and solving problems.

The intuitive function is to explore possibilities and to see the truth directly.

Self-image is the product of the intellect, a picture in the computer.

Feelings are the energy context of meaning.

Awareness is the light by which we see.

Will is the ability to direct energy this way or that.

High thinking is discriminatory—separate from intellect but connected to it.

And "I" am a living soul, the one who "owns" all the functions.

It is okay to think, feel, desire, remember, or do anything—just so it is not done " in sleep." Enlightenment is not concentration on the now, nor is it only sensate awareness. It is simple awareness. That is all.

GOD IS; I AM; WE ARE

"I" am a light shining brightly
a here/now presence
indivisible into parts
an energy animating a body
a body emanating spiritual energy
a living intelligence
a freedom amid conditioning
the one who sees through these eyes.
And God: Where is God?
God is in the Self.
The Self is in God.

And yet, the Self is not-God:
It knows not the secrets of the universe;
it creates not its own existence;
it has no power beyond its own freedom
    and knowledge;
it exists only in a limited sphere.
God and I are not-one, not-two.
"God is"; "I am"; "We are."

*Can't find yourself? Just open
your eyes! There you are: looking!*

THE SEEING "I"

The eyes of the "I" are like windows.
Who peers through them?
An old, familiar Soul;
an infant, waking up—.
Me! Just-me! That is all.
And what I see, I see without illusion—
    fresh, clean, here, now.
There is no interpretation, no judgment, no projection,
    no conceptual filtering.
There is just-me and whatever I am looking at—
    and this is the universe.
It is beautiful!
That which God has created is very, very good.
The one who sees is good; that which is seen is good;
    the seeing is good.

There is nothing to fear. This moment is all there is. It is
Eternal Life.

*T*he eyes are windows. Who is peering
out of them? Just look! Don't analyze.
There is nothing to know. See with your
eyes, not your intellect. Let things be.
This is the way to experience the
simplicity of existence. Experience
this, but do not try to define it.

I AM

"I am" is the affirmation of the fact of my existence as a person. It is also God's affirmation of existence as a person.

Only a person can say and know the meaning of "I am."

To attempt to define or explain "I am" is to reduce it and annihilate the mystery. Do not say, "I am a husband" or "I am a writer." Rather say, "I husband" or "I write."

Personhood is not something I do, neither is it here or there. It is who I am, and it is in every cell of my body.

Be a person. Rest in the mystery "That I am."

The direct, nonconceptual, unmediated experience of the "I" is what Zen calls enlightenment. It is a spiritual experience because the "I" is a direct creation of God; it cannot be derived from other states.

In Christian faith, the "I" realizes that it, too, is seen and chosen by another "I," the Father who sees all, including the "I" whom the Father has created through his Logos, or Christ.

Christian enlightenment is the experience of the mystical, transcendent "Thou" of God by an awakened "I." Through Christian enlightenment, then, we become not only awake but also a person—one who *"belongs to* God" and who can give and receive love. Christian enlightenment is what all people hunger for.

*No self-definition, no ego. Allow God
to define you, and you will know yourself.*

CHRISTIAN ENLIGHTENMENT

Enlightenment is the natural, awakened state of a person. It happens of its own accord when one lives unintentionally in the NOW.

Nonintentional living happens when the disturbance of judgmental thinking is dropped.

Judgmental thinking is dropped when the past is healed through forgiveness and, after prudent planning, the future is left to itself. One must also make many decisions to drop unnecessary thinking and to never judge as good or bad that which is neither good nor bad—except in reference to the ego.

All this may be done outside of the context of formal religious practices. In fact, formal religious practices could possibly serve to negate this liberation.

Enlightenment is not love, and it is not mystical contemplation, for these are experienced in relationship. Rather enlightenment is the perfect context for relationship since self-centered projections and demands are out of the way. Love flowers most beautifully in the good soils of an enlightened Soul!

Enlightenment is the loss of the experience of the reflective, intentional Self. There is no longer a sense of a solid or "boundaried" Self, and yet there is the other who is "not-me." There are also all these actions I do, for which I must take responsibility.

And so the intellect affirms that even in enlightenment, there is an individual agent of choice who is not the other. Neither is this choosing a robotic spinning out of conditioning. Were that the case, one would be less free in enlightenment than before.

If robotic conditioning is not doing the choosing, and the reflective, intentional ego is not doing the choosing, then who is making the choices I make all day long, and what is the process by which such choices are made?

It seems as though the right action emerges spontaneously in response to the needs of the moment.

Who responds?

Hush now, or you'll fall asleep.

*B*e ye enlightened, O Christian brothers
and sisters! Accept the gift of the East. Be
here/now, and love will be born.

THE COMING OF ENLIGHTENMENT

Live the Great Sermon, and enlightenment will come in due time. The specific contributions Jesus makes unto this end are

- his constant, supportive friendship
- his Spirit within, to renew and configure the soul in his own image
- his Flesh and Blood, to graft us into his Mystical Body and order our energies accordingly
- his own knowledge of the Creator as Personal, Loving Being
- his Church—other people with whom to journey and celebrate
- sound teaching, to strengthen and properly orient the mind

We have here a Master through whom the whole universe will be renewed. Only he can bear the full vision and live as human flesh.

Who among the Eastern masters can equal Christ?

Entrust your soul to him and him alone. The others can give you only what they know, which is in no way superior to the enlightenment of Christ.

"Do as he tells you," Our Lady said.

N ever, ever stop believing that you are!
If you are not, then who is there to accept
responsibility for your behavior?
God?
Absurd!
The conditioned mind?
Whose conditioned mind?
Yours!

CHRIST: GOD'S SELF-IMAGE

The objective pole of Self is the self-image/self-concept, or the ego.

The subjective pole cannot be seen, for it is the see-er. Nevertheless, its characteristics are freedom, mystery, and personality, meaning a capacity to love.

The objective Self is awake to particularity. The subjective Self is awake at the level of existence, oneness. The energetic bond between the two is libido, or psychic energy.

God's subjectivity is the Father. God's objectification is the universe and, especially, the Son, who is the Image of the unseen (but seeing) God. Christ is God's Self-image, as it were. Through him, we come to that mysterious Subjectivity who is the Person Jesus called Father. The energy bond between Father and Son is the Spirit, who testifies to both.

Jesus knew all of the above. In him, human and divine

subjectivity and objectivity were one. To see him is to see the divine image in human form. To behold his gaze is to see the personal quality of his human/divine soul. To grow close to him is to become like him—to know what he knows as he knows.

Y*our being is an "eye" through which God sees creation. God wants to know creation in and through you. In doing so, you come to see with God's seeing, know with God's knowing, love with God's loving. This is the meaning of incarnational spirituality.*

ABOUT GOD

About God, believe only

- that God exists in a realm transcendent to what the senses can perceive. This realm includes the interiority of the soul
- that God creates this world through atoms, molecules, cells, and organs, and gives consciousness as the creative force and guidance within all these levels
- that God only loves. The pains of growth and injustice do not negate this reality
- that Christ is God-incarnate, taking on our nature
- that evolution now unfolds "in-Christ." With Christ, a new evolutionary epoch has begun
- that Christ and the Father are bonded in the Holy Spirit, whose presence within guides and transforms our own human spirits

- that Eucharist is Christ's risen body and the medium through which Christ becomes enfleshed in humans
- that, therefore, God is to be trusted, loved, and enjoyed as both dual and nondual Partner

*W*hy *do I love You? Why do*
You love me? How can there be two,
happy as we?" Just because!

THAT-I-AM

The soul is the source of mind and body. It is also expressed as mind and body. Body and mind are contained in the Soul.

The essence of the Soul is awareness and freedom. These are spiritual qualities that can be experienced directly in deep silence. Most of us, however, experience them indirectly by means of the operations of the spirit through mind and body.

The direct experience of the Soul-self is "That I am." This is qualitatively different from the experience of "Who I am," which is the ego self. The knowledge "That I am" allows us great inner freedom and a sense of the unity of all things. It also awakens in us a sense "That God is," for my "That-ness" is received in each moment from God. This sense of God, however, becomes more explicit and personal through faith and prayer.

To know "That I am" is to know immortality. "That-ness" is not a consequence of the flesh, which will pass away. "That I am" does not come and go. It always "Is."

*T*he *"I" who sees cannot be defined,*
but it can be experienced. Enjoy it,
and there "you" are.

THE NATURE OF THE SOUL

Although the Christian spiritual journey is primarily focused on the relationship between a person and God, it is helpful to have a Christian understanding of the nature of the Soul. This is especially desirable today when many people are attracted to Eastern or metaphysical views of human nature that are at odds with Christianity. Many seem to be unaware that Christianity, too, has come to a deep and comprehensive metaphysical understanding of human nature. This understanding can help us make sense of the true meaning of spirituality.

The Christian view of the Soul: The following points should not be taken as a summary of Christian metaphysics but simply as a listing of some of the distinctive features of the Christian view of the Soul:

1. The Soul is a spiritual reality oriented toward animating matter to form a body. With other spirits, it shares these characteristics:

   a. *Simplicity.* The Soul is one indivisible whole with no parts. It contains the physical body, which it informs to the smallest atom to make the body live. It also contains faculties of reason, will, memory, and so forth; but these are not divisions of the Soul—only faculties to enable its operations.

   b. *Immortality.* Other life forms are said to have a vegetative soul (plant life, animal physiology) and/or animal soul (life of the senses, instinctive reactions). These souls are perishable. The spiritual Soul of a human being contains the vegetative and animal souls and is responsible for their existence and functioning. At death, however, the vegetative and animal levels cease to exist in a human being, since they are fundamentally oriented to the life of the physical body, which is left behind at death.

c. *Immateriality.* The Soul is a spiritual substance and, as such, is immortal. Nevertheless, it is a spirit that is meant to give life to a physical body and to exercise itself in a body.

d. *Freedom.* The Soul may choose to do this or that. These choices are limited by the information available.

e. *Intelligence.* Like angels, the Soul is capable of grasping spiritual truth directly through intuition. It may also gain knowledge through the exercise of reason from information obtained from the senses.

f. *Personal.* Each Soul is individual, belonging to the individual, whose intellectual and volitional experiences are possessed by that individual. This characteristic is responsible for the experience of self-consciousness.

g. *Creatureliness.* The Soul is a creation of God. It is not eternal; rather, it is created directly by God at conception. Therefore, the Soul is not a divine substance, although it is dependent on God for its existence and is, therefore, connected with God because of its existence.

2. Without a body, the spiritual Soul is metaphysically deficient, for the intelligence and exercising of the characteristics of the Soul described above are oriented toward life in a body. This is why a complete restoration of the Soul calls for a body in and through which the Soul may express itself. A human Soul differs from an angelic spirit in this regard, for an angelic spirit is created to know and express itself in a purely spiritual state of being.

3. When the spiritual Soul was first given, its contact with the Divine was such that its energy was infused with divine energy so that the animal, vegetative, and physical

levels were taken up into the immortality of the spiritual Soul. With the Fall, however, the Soul maintained its spiritual nature, but its energy was no longer infused with the divine energy. Consequentially, the body lost the immortality infused by the spiritual Soul and became destined for death.

4. As a spirit, the Soul may live apart from the body in the afterlife. This is called the intermediate state of the Soul. During this phase of its journey, the Soul experiences all of the qualities of spirits listed above. So the Soul intuitively comprehends its relationship with God and others, thus entering into either hell, purgatory, or heaven.

5. Although the usual manner of knowing for the Soul is through the body and information gained from the senses, it is nonetheless possible for the embodied Soul to experience its spiritual nature while in the body. Thus it is that philosophers sometimes speak of two experiences of the Soul:

   a. *The corporal Soul.* The normal state of the Soul in this life. Its rational and intuitive intelligence is ultimately derived from sensory information and directed toward actions to be performed by the body.

   b. *The partly body-free Soul.* As a spirit, the Soul is not completely contained by the life and needs of the body. It reaches beyond the body and may experience some of the qualities of a pure spirit, although imperfectly. The partly body-free Soul explains such phenomena as extrasensory perception, cosmic consciousness, spiritual travel (astral body travel), occult phenomena, and natural mysticism (for example, some forms of Eastern spirituality).

Certain ascetical practices can loosen the hold of the Soul on the physical body so that it may experience its spiritual nature in this manner. In this state, the Soul may realize its connection with God as the giver of existence and so obtain a kind of natural, nonpersonal union with God. This seems to be the kind of experience that practitioners of certain Eastern spiritualities tend toward. Such spiritualities explore the powers of the Soul and lead their adherents, through a life of moral living and ascetical discipline, to realize this natural union between the Soul and its Maker. This natural, or metaphysical, mysticism is obviously different from the relational spirituality described in the Judeo-Christian tradition, although it is certainly not without merit and should by no means be considered diabolical.

In this state, too, the Soul may sometimes communicate with angelic, demonic, and disembodied spirits who may, in turn, communicate to the physical realm through the faculties of the spiritual Soul. This is the basis for channeling (necromancy) and spiritualism, both of which are condemned by the Church, since it is unlikely that good spirits would be involved in such communications. This may also explain some of the dynamics of demonic possession.

It frequently happens that a Christian mystic, too, will be drawn to this state, wherein the Soul will enjoy ecstatic union with God or receive communication from God without going through the usual channels of sensation and conceptualization.

This is called *infused contemplation,* a deep union of love between God and the Soul made possible by grace.

The partly body-free Soul may also explain manifestations of extrasensory preternatural powers. Such powers need not be attributed to angels, demons, or disembodied spirits, but may belong to the Soul itself. Generally, these powers lie dormant in the unconscious or superconscious mind. In the partly body-free state, however, they may manifest in certain individuals. This explanation accounts for the unpredictability of these gifts and the inability of the person to produce them at will.

6. As a created spirit, the Soul naturally longs for union with its Maker even while it infuses life into the body. The fundamental dispositions of the Soul, then, are twofold:

    a. To give life to the body and thus cultivate its spiritual powers in a context of embodied life to which the Soul is properly suited (unlike angels and demons, which are not suited for embodiment)
    b. To be united with God, its source of life and existence. Catholic theology does not see an opposition between these two dispositions. The body and its needs do not negate the spiritual life of the Soul. The body is not a prison of the Soul nor an obstacle to union with God. Nevertheless, a Soul too attached to bodily life cannot be united with God—nor can a Soul who rejects the life of the body. A sound spiritual approach recognizes the importance of proper and disciplined care for the body and its needs while cultivating union with God.

*H*appiness is unconditioned
consciousness. Stop disturbing yourself
and you will be happy.

HAPPINESS AND THE TRUE SELF

There are many problems in life; the world is unrelenting in its assault. For example, there is sickness, death, rain, floods, tornadoes. If any of these are not happening, there is always the risk.

The tragedy is to reserve being okay until there are no problems. Even were such a goal reached, there would be the dynamic of "I'll be okay when..." to contend with, as it focuses now on preventing problems.

No! There is only to accept the inevitable and do what has to be done—here/now/in-love. Living in the True Self is the pearl of great price, and it is not contingent on the absence of problems. Its only conditions are present-moment awareness, an open heart, conceptual open-mindedness, and a willingness to be grown anew by God.

There is no happiness in physical health, material prosperity, or rational conceptualization. Only in total surrender to God is salvation known.

Only Love is happiness. The higher states of consciousness do not bring happiness except insofar as they express Love.

Therefore, the only way to live is to stand completely naked in this moment, with no crutches or attachments, willing to give and receive life, allowing the Spirit to form you. This nakedness must be whole body-mind-spirit, so that attention is not identified with any level of consciousness but diffused into them all. There must be no self-contraction, no defensiveness, no preconceptions. Breathe deeply, accepting life and returning it holistically.

This is poverty of spirit—to cling to nothing while permitting God's action within. Only when we are in this condition can Love do its mysterious work. Only when we are in this condition can the True Self be realized.

No need for anxiety! All is well in God. The worst that can happen cannot undo this truth.

THE "WAY" TO HAPPINESS

My "way," or "logic," of happiness can best be summarized as follows:

- If you're going to be alive anyway, why be miserable? Why not be as happy as possible every moment of the day?
- If there is heaven, then your happiness goes on and on. If not, then is it not still better to pass the time in joy than in sadness?
- If you would be happy, then you must also learn about what happiness is and what stops you from being happy.
- What stops you from being happy is the belief that you lack something necessary for happiness. You have placed a condition on happiness and you perceive that condition to be lacking.
- Unhappiness is conditioned, judgmental, rejecting of the NOW, self-focused.
- If unhappiness is so, then happiness cannot exist unless this situation is reversed. Happiness must be something that is unconditioned, nonjudgmental, accepting of the NOW, loving.
- Only God is unconditioned, nonjudgmental, NOW, loving.
- To be happy is to be like God.
- To be like God, you must be with-God.
- To be with-God, you must be where God is, when God is there, as God is there.
- Since God is always-here/now/as-love, to be happy, you must be-here/now/in-love.
- God is here.
- God is NOW.

- God is loving everyone and everything without judgment or reserve.
- Where are you?
- What are you doing?
- What are you waiting for?

So far as I can see, there is no other way for me to be happy but to love and serve my family, and to place myself at their disposal for their growth. That cared for—an enormous task, to be sure—the same goes for my larger family, the Church. I am here to serve with my gifts and talents, to help others grow.

The same goes for the whole human race and the planet. I am a vessel through which God's love may flow. This is my happiness and my work. It is God who has forged me into this vessel that I might enjoy the sanity and blessedness of giving.

*L ook around you. Everything is
creation-manifesting-God, if only you
have eyes to see and a heart to feel.*

REALITY, SANITY, AND WISDOM

True knowledge is *both* one and many.

Intuition and feeling know the unitive aspect. Sensory information and reason focus on particularity.

The rational Self knows God as Thou. The intuitive, feeling Self knows God as the very light of the Soul.

I think, I choose: essence.

Beyond thinking and choosing: existence.

Do choice and conceptualization cease with the experience of unity?

Life goes on but without a willful agent. The "I" is there, but nonasserting. The "I" enjoys and continues to know that it must be a particularity, for it is not privy to the thoughts and feelings of others and cannot will for them. Those who say particularity is an illusion are themselves deluded.

When existence is realized, the illusion of particularity as ultimate truth is lost. Particularity in unity is realized. Now life will begin!

True sanity comes not from intellectual certainty or self-assurance (which is almost always contrived), but from unrelenting self-honesty in loving acceptance.

Ultimately, you are a mystery, at-one-with-God and so undefinable.

The only true sanity is to be found in honestly accepting what you are experiencing now as you struggle to be lovingly engaged in the reality of the moment. It's okay to remember and plan, but no nostalgia, and no projecting.

You do not possess sanity. Rather, God is your sanity. You are sane—even when in pain—when you surrender to the inevitable in love.

Abandon yourself to the care of God. If your brain gets sick or your organ systems make you mentally unstable, that is dis-ease, not insanity. Christ will preserve you and renew you in the end.

True wisdom is walking in the way of Christ. Then will understanding be given. The temptation is to get the conceptual paradigm all defined and then to live out its implications. This is the thorn of the mental ego.

The truth is that we do not really know conceptually what *is*. We only know from revelation that it is friendly, creative loving—personal.

Conceptualization is a way of organizing information in the service of language. It is also a kind of understanding, and it can point attention in the right direction. Beyond this, however, it is of no use. Once you see the moon, you must quit looking at the finger that points to it and quit reading what the blind say about it. You simply look, and the understanding comes of its own accord.

Can the butterfly be seen in the cater-pillar? Not by other caterpillars, it cannot. It can be seen only with butterfly eyes.

DESTINY AND CONTROL

You do not know what God has created. You do not possess full knowledge of your potentialities. Therefore, it is best to remain open to your own, continuing unfolding, destiny.

Do not limit your possibilities through a narrow projecting of your giftedness and self-image, however. Instead, follow the lead of your heart.

Allow your destiny to unfold of its own accord. Set no rigid goals about where you "should be" in five years. Simply continue to develop your talents one day at a time, here/now/in-love." The Spirit will lead you where you are needed and where you may grow. God knows what God has created, and God will bring you to fruition.

Remember that you control nothing! Nothing! You could die tonight. You could get a brain disease and go insane. Your spouse and/or children could die, get sick, or become disturbed. The economy could fail, leaving you destitute. The nations could war and destroy the environment that supports you. You could be fired from your job or find yourself working for an incompetent boss.

You can prevent none of these from happening. If they do not happen, it is grace, or luck, and you should be grateful. The only control you have is in your willingness to be here/

now/in-love. Sick or healthy, this you can do. All the rest is circumstantial, contingent, and unpredictable.

If you do not know what to do, then wait for the answer in openness, cherishing the questions in gentleness.

SPIRITUAL GROWTH

From beginning to end, the process of growth lies outside the range of our capacity to exercise absolute control. From the production of gametes to the fertilization of the egg to the division of the zygote to cellular differentiation to organic homeostasis, through Erikson's, Loevinger's, Kohlberg's, Maslow's, and Piaget's stages of growth to recovery from sicknesses to energy upheavals and resolutions to death and beyond: We do not possess the ability to control these movements of life.

We may affect the growth process—usually for the worse—through the exercise of will: trying to make ourselves into someone, in our own image and likeness. We may also experience our own unfolding and marvel at what is happening.

Therefore, the best course of action is always complete surrender and docility to the growth process. This "way" is not always clear, of course, but it will reveal itself if we are willing to follow the path of love, serenity, and truth. Is this not, in the end, precisely the Way?

It is God who grows us through the dynamic of needs and their fulfillment. Dependent creatures, we experience our neediness for a wide number of things. The manner in which we meet these needs determines what kind of people we become. Our needs change as we grow, and so we continue pursuing them, changing and evolving as we do so.

There is a general tendency to need less if the journey proceeds along moral lines. Simplicity is the mark of a saint. Fresh water, wholesome food, a roof, a fire, a few friends, Eucharist, times for silence, meaningful work—these are of the essence and there is no disposing of them without seriously impairing the quality of life.

Meet your needs in a healthy, loving manner, and help others to do so as well. Feel your needs and don't try to force your growth in any direction. Simply live well, and your growth will unfold of its own accord.

The surest sign of spiritual health is to be found in your ability to take an interest in other people, to really listen to them, and to be willing to help them in whatever manner is appropriate. When your spirituality does not produce this fruit, you are probably involved in delusions of some kind.

3

SPIRITUALITY AND THE HUMAN CONDITION

When you read, do so with an open
mind and in a spirit of detachment.
Receive the words deep in your heart
but do not hold on to them. Notice
your questions; welcome them, hold
on to them, and let them bring forth
their truth in due time.

now that we have more clarity about what
we mean by the terms Self, Soul, and God, we are able to
reflect on how our human nature has become wounded,
and the consequences we suffer from this.

We begin again with definitions, this time of the ego—a
term that is used in many different ways by psychologists and
spiritual writers. Some consider the ego to be a false or illu-

sory Self but, for purposes of this work, I will use the term as Carl Jung and many others have done; I will use "ego" to refer to the conscious aspect of the Self. In this sense, we might say that the Self is, for most of us, still largely unconscious, and the ego is its conscious representative. Sometimes the image of an iceberg is used to show this relationship: the Self being the whole iceberg and the ego being the part of the Self that is above the water, or conscious and awake in space and time. The ego stands between the outside world and the unconscious, arbitrating how these two realms interact.

The form, or "shape," the ego takes is usually identified with *self-image*. What is self-image?

- Self-image is the picture we have of ourselves as a result of our life experiences. When we focus this picture into the realm of thought, we can speak of *self-concept*. Self-concept is our idea of ourselves; self-image is the picture of this idea.

- Self-image/concept arises from

  1. *Groups and labels we are identified with:* American, Catholic, Kansan, Cardinals fan, St. Romain. When someone comments on these groups, we are affected.
  2. *Our roles:* mother, husband, brother, counselor, minister, son, and so forth. These roles give us a sense of identity.
  3. *Our self-judgments:* pretty, intelligent, tall, stubborn. When someone's opinions conflict with our own self-judgments, we are deeply affected.
  4. *Others' judgments:* This may be identical with our own self-judgments, or there may be differences.

Self-image, then, is what gives the ego its form, or structure. The ego makes its choices by referring to self-image. If, for example, a friend asks me to take a ballet class with her, I project my self-image into this possibility. I may say, "I can't see myself doing that." I am saying that the picture I have of myself does not do ballet dancing. When people say, "This is who I am," they are usually referring to self-image.

THE EGO AND
THE UNCONSCIOUS SELF

Although most people identify their ego as their whole Self, we know this cannot be true. There are hours and hours of every day when we do not even experience the ego. For example, there is no ego experience when we sleep—except during dreams. Yet we know that a Self still exists when we sleep, for if someone calls our name, we wake up. It is a deeper level of Self that recognizes our name during sleep. Then it is Self that begins to function as ego after we wake up.

We must recognize, therefore, a second aspect of Self—an unconscious, nonegoic dimension. The intentionality of this *unconscious Self* may be quite a bit different from ego. The unconscious Self wants harmony and wholeness for the whole person. What the ego wants might be something altogether different—something that brings the person into disharmony and fragmentation. Hence, we frequently find a conflict between the ego and the unconscious Self.

The language of the ego is that of the culture. Dreams, spontaneous fantasies, and intuitive hunches are the language of the unconscious Self. It is through such nonverbal language that the unconscious Self tries to communicate with the ego.

We have noted that it is the unconscious Self that hears and recognizes our names when we sleep. We now note that it is also the unconscious Self that knows and recognizes the presence of God. Deep within, this unconscious Self is already attuned to the presence of God, for it is God who gives life to the Self in each moment. The striving for wholeness by the unconscious Self is "*in*-formed," we might say, by its awareness of God. This is not to say, as the Hindus do, that the unconscious Self is God, or Atman. God is the One who gives the Self its existence. The Self is the one who is aware of being given existence by God.

*E*very person is a Self-becoming. If you
know this for yourself, you will see it
in others.

HUMAN BROKENNESS: HOW WE LOSE CONTACT WITH GOD

When we are born, there is no ego; there is only the unconscious Self expressing itself through a limited number of instinctive behaviors. This unconscious Self is also attuned to its environment in a feeling way. As infants, we can tell whether we are loved or rejected. As we develop, we are shaped by our environment at the level of emotion. Within a few months, we begin to understand something of the meaning of the words we are hearing. By the age of two, we understand many words, including the words *me* and *mine*. At this stage, the human subject is capable of perceiving himself or herself as an object of attention. This is the beginning of the ego.

In a perfect world, where everyone unconditionally loves everyone else, the ego would exist in a beautiful harmony with the unconscious Self. This unconscious Self would, in turn, be a medium through which God's presence would always be informing the decisions of the ego. As we all know, this is not the situation in which we find ourselves.

Instead, what we find is disharmony between the concerns of the ego and the deeper Self. Consequently, the ego has lost its "natural" sense of God's presence and feels alienated from God. We are more awake to the concerns of ego than to the presence of God, which is a sure sign that something has gone wrong.

How did this happen to us? Here is a hypothetical scenario:

1. The environment in which we grow up loves us conditionally. This begins in the womb, where the developing embryo is attuned to the emotional state of the mother and, through her, to the rest of the world. Later, the care we receive from our parents and family communicates *conditional love* in many ways.

2. When we, the embryo—and later the infant—is loved conditionally, we experience at least a slight sense of rejection and the emotion of fear. If we are loved very little, there is great fear and distrust very deep within.

3. As the ego begins to develop, the emotional consequences of conditional love—mostly fear, distrust, and shame—create a turmoil in the unconscious that prevents the ego from developing in harmony with the unconscious Self. It is as if the light of God mediated through the unconscious Self is blocked out by these deep emotional scars. Hence, the ego will be much more attuned to the outside world and will be in some kind of avoidance posture toward the inner world of the unconscious as it develops.

4. The ideas and images of ourselves that we pick up from the developmental environment reinforce our feeling of being loved conditionally. In many ways, we learn that we are loved for what we do, not for who we are. At the level of thought, therefore, we conclude that we are conditionally lovable and acceptable. Our self-judgment and our

perception of others' judgments of us—two integral parts of self-image—are deeply colored by this conditionality.

5. Concluding that we are only conditionally lovable and acceptable, we are constantly on the alert for the conditions by which we can become more acceptable to ourselves and others. These conditions are perceived to exist in externals—in the opinions of others, in accomplishments, in money and other possessions. The center of attention of the ego, then, is drawn to the outside world as the source of happiness.

6. Having lost touch with the presence of God in the ground of our deepest Self, the ego has also lost its true identity. To compensate, the ego identifies strongly with family roles, nation, race, athletic heroes, and other people to gain for itself some kind of identity through association.

This, then, is a brief summary of how we become split within ourselves through the experience of conditional love. Since everyone grows up in an environment of conditional love, everyone experiences this kind of brokenness and loss of contact with God. There are a wide range of possibilities here, since some environments are much more loving than others. To the extent that we have not been loved for who we are, however, we are damaged.

A little actor on the stage: the False Self (including the Christian mental ego).

THE FALSE SELF: SICKNESS OF SOUL

Out of this condition of being wounded and broken, we develop *a False Self*. This False Self is a whole dimension of the personality, encompassing both egoic and unconscious levels.

It is not the whole of the personality, however. Were that so, we would be incapable of seeing the reality of our condition, and we would never be able to change. Nevertheless, the degree of infection by the False Self system is very pervasive. It is like a cancer that has spread throughout the entire Soul, although it has not completely killed the Soul. The deepest, unconscious self-center remains free from contamination by the False Self.

What is this False Self like? Let us list a few of its characteristics by summarizing its philosophy of life.

- I am conditionally lovable and acceptable. I have no real worth in and of myself. *I must do something to be loved and accepted.* My worth is predicated on doing the right things.
- The conditions for getting love and acceptance are defined by people and circumstances outside myself. Therefore, I must use my rational intelligence to constantly scan the culture and the opinions of others to perceive the conditions by which I will attain a sense of worth and meaning. I am constantly judging other people and circumstances according to my perceived conditions for happiness.
- I will do whatever is necessary to gain the approval of others, all the while avoiding their disapproval. I will reveal those aspects of myself to others that I think they want to see; for if they knew what I really thought and felt, they might not accept me.
- The God I believe in is utterly transcendent—totally outside of myself. Like everything else, I have to do certain things the right way in order to gain God's approval. Religion teaches me what these right things are.

- When I feel numb or painful inside as a result of living according to this philosophy, I will use mood-altering "fixes" to make myself feel better or to take the edge off my inner pain.

Anyone can see that this philosophy of life is laden with many pitfalls. Few people are free of this consciousness, however, because as already noted, there are both conscious and unconscious aspects to this False Self system. Also, for many people, this False Self is so dominant and so caught up in external concerns that they are little aware of anything else.

The False Self system is responsible for all our misery and for the destruction of the planet. It is totally out of touch with the harmonizing influences of the deeper Self, so it is constantly trying to change the external world and external circumstances in an attempt to gain happiness. Because our happiness is within and is not a consequence of adequate external factors, the False Self only succeeds in creating disharmony in the world. This disharmony has brought the planet to a state of crisis!

Working as a system of consciousness at the level of the ego and the unconscious, the False Self—like all other states of consciousness—operates out of a certain intentionality, or center. This center, we have noted, is a spiritual issue.

So what is the center, or intentionality, of the False Self? It is looking outward to other people, things, or circumstances to make us happy. This is its general orientation, fired by the intellectual and emotional convictions that, in and of ourselves, we are flawed, a mistake, unlovable, and unacceptable. We think we must accomplish something or get something to be loved, so we are always looking outside ourselves to discover what this might be. We call this external referencing.

Specifically, this external referencing is usually focused on one source as most responsible for our happiness—and most commonly this is another person. We tell ourselves that we cannot be okay without that person's good opinion of us, without his or her approval, without being special to that person. Sometimes it is not one person but a group of people (maybe the whole world) that we are trying to impress. When we do succeed in getting this approval, we feel high, thrilled, exalted. It is like a drug. The more we get, the more we want.

Of course, the shadow side of this is that when these external sources do not give us approval, we feel low, devastated, down on ourselves. As a result of depending on other people in this way for our happiness, we lose the freedom to really be ourselves before others. We are constantly wondering—to the point of preoccupation—what they think of us, draining the psyche of energies that could be used for other purposes.

What I have just described is *relationship addiction,* or *codependency.* It is but one possible manifestation of the False Self system. External referencing might also be focused in work, accomplishments, sex, gambling, winning, food, television, alcohol and drugs, shopping, and a wide range of other mood-altering possibilities. Any and all of these can be used addictively and can become full-blown addictions in their own right.

In a real sense, then, the False Self system is an addictive Self. Here are a few conclusions which force themselves upon us at this point:

1. Addictive fixes are the center on which the False Self focuses. Addiction, then, is primarily a spiritual concern. It is the "spirituality" of the False Self giving rise, like all spiritualities, to a particular way of life and bringing a particular quality of energy and awareness to the one who lives this life. This way of life, its energy, and the attentional state it expresses all belong to the False Self.
2. Everyone has been loved conditionally and has developed a False Self to compensate for this. Only Jesus Christ and his mother, Mary, are excluded from this disease.

3. Everyone is an addict. The question is, what kind? Some, myself included, use a wide variety of things as fixes; some of us use only one or two.
4. The False Self system with its addictive preoccupations is the primary obstacle to experiencing God's presence.

This is putting the matter quite bluntly, I realize, and few people want to admit that they are addicts. But if we are to grow in Christian spirituality, the truth of the fourth point cannot be overstated. If we would come to center our lives in Christ, then we must also recognize that there is much about us that will resist the changes in lifestyle that Christian spirituality calls for. Let us identify the False Self system right from the beginning as the source of this resistance. The False Self is that which is within us that resists Christ. Using other, more theological terms, Saint Paul called it the presence of sin living in himself. (See Romans 7:15-25.)

I am sometimes greatly disturbed by the prevalent attitude that this False Self system is "natural." It is *not* natural! It is, however, common. God did not create people to become False Selves. The False Self is a perversion of what God has created. Its centers of meaning and values have nothing to do with God's will.

In the following pages, you will be invited to get in touch with the presence of this False Self in your own life. The purpose of these exercises is not to get you down on yourself but to help you begin to see the False Self for what it is and what it does to you. By beginning to see the False Self in this way, you will be awakening the *True Self* within. The True Self is that which is within us that sees the False Self for what it is and is attuned to the energies of the Spirit of God. To empower the True Self to understand the nature of the False Self; we are already moving deeper into a conversion process, or spiritual awakening.

In our growth in Christian spirituality, then, we want to

come closer and closer to the Lord. Recognizing the False Self as the obstacle to this closeness, out of our love of the Lord, we become intent on naming it and letting it go. Every time we let go of a little bit of the False Self system we experience greater detachment, freedom, and serenity.

> *The False Self system is a mental-conceptual organization of life experiences and memories focused around a general emotional theme or motive, that is, security, power, pleasure, recognition, and so on.*

CHARACTERISTICS OF THE FALSE SELF SYSTEM

Consider the characteristics of the False Self system listed below. For each one that applies to you, write on a separate sheet of paper or in your personal journal how you experience this characteristic in your everyday life and what consequences you and others suffer because of it.

1. I am more in touch with what I want for my life than with what God wants for my life.
2. I frequently feel numb, empty, or cranky.
3. I am afraid to discover what's really going on deep inside myself, and I try to avoid this by living on a more superficial level.
4. When I become uncomfortable inside myself, I find some way to escape from this discomfort by using television, food, work, a relationship, alcohol, drugs, shopping, gambling, reading material, religious activities, or chatter.

5. I am often critical of myself.

6. I am often critical of others.

7. My mind is often filled with anxious preoccupations about the future and about whether I will be able to get or keep what I think I need.

8. It is difficult for me to just *be*. I generally feel that I must be *doing something* to justify my life to myself.

9. I am trying to find happiness by getting something I don't have or by getting rid of something I do have but don't want.

10. In relationships with others, I generally feel I have to play a role or wear a mask. If I do not do this, others will probably reject me.

11. I frequently do not even know what my true thoughts and feelings are.

12. My self-concept or idea of myself is skewed so that I see myself as inferior to others or I see myself as superior to others.

13. I am constantly comparing myself to others to determine if I am "ahead" of them or "behind" them in some area of life.

14. When people insult or ridicule something or someone I identify with, I feel personally insulted and become angry. (For example, when my country is criticized, I become defensive.)

15. The roles I play give me a sense of identity. What I do is who I am. If I could not continue to do what I do, I would not know who I am.

16. When someone criticizes the way I do something, I feel personally put down. I have a hard time separating what I do from my identity.

17. It seems that all my thoughts, feelings, memories, and desires are related to my self-image—to changing it or to maintaining it.

18. If I could better control the people and external circumstances in my life, I would be happier.
19. I tend to view close friends and family members as "mine." I tend to treat them that way, too.
20. I tend to view God as judgmental. I believe I have to do the right things—usually religious kinds of behavior—to win God's approval. I seldom feel that I am in harmony with God.
21. It is hard for me to see how God is involved in the everyday affairs of my life. Generally, it seems that God has nothing to do with me and my life. God has better things to do.
22. In my prayer, I spend more time asking God to do what I want than praying for the grace to do what God wants.

There is no such thing as "self-possession." The only Self that is stable is the one that emerges in ongoing loving surrender, for this Self can never be taken away.

INVENTORY OF INORDINATE DESIRES AND DELUSIONS

Answer the following questions in the blanks on the following pages, on a separate sheet of paper, or in a personal journal. In answering the questions, consider your physical health, relationships, present occupation, material comforts, emotional health, your sense of God's presence—anything!

Desires

1. To want what I do not have! What is this for me?

   a.

   b.

   c.

   d.

   e.

2. There are conditions and circumstances in my life that I am rejecting: I have what I do not want! What are these conditions and circumstances?

   a.

   b.

   c.

   d.

   e.

Delusions

1. On a thinking level, how do my desires reinforce the attitude "I'll be okay when..."?

2. Which of the following are true for me? I'll be okay when
   a. other people like me.
   b. I have good physical health.
   c. I retire.
   d. I have more money.
   e. I have more time to myself.
   f. The bishop (my spouse/boss/child) does what he/she is supposed to do.
   g. (Add your own personal statements.)

ADDICTIVE BEHAVIORS CHECKLIST

Notice the "Addictive Behaviors" listed below and the set of statements that follows. On a separate sheet of paper or in a personal journal write the list of "Addictive Behaviors" as it appears below. Next to each of the addictive behaviors, indicate the number of the statement that makes an accurate observation about your own conduct.

Addictive behaviors

Alcohol/drug intake	Working
Overeating/undereating	Gambling
Approval-seeking	Religious activities
Taking care of others	Watching television
Sexual expression	Shopping

1. When I am feeling down, I frequently turn to this activity to feel better.
2. I am uncomfortable with the way I indulge myself in this behavior.

3. I sometimes lie about my involvement in this behavior.
4. When I go without this activity for a while, I feel uncomfortable and panicky.
5. My behavior in this area causes problems for me (physical, relational, and so on).
6. My behavior in this area causes problems for others.
7. I have tried to stop this behavior, but I inevitably go back to it.
8. When others confront me about this behavior, I become defensive.
9. Because of this behavior, I have cut back on healthy involvements.
10. If I could better control myself in this area, my life would be more manageable.

A number next to any of these behaviors may indicate an addictive involvement. The more numbers for any behavior, the more intense the addictive involvement.

Do you believe God's will is your happiness? If not, then whose will is?

A LITANY OF HOPE FOR THE SICK SOUL

A diseased body can be easily defined in terms of failure in organ systems and tissues.

A diseased mind is weak, confused, undisciplined, attached to many things, a volcano of negative thoughts and emotions.

A sick soul is hopeless.

The body and mind cannot heal when the spirit is hopeless. Any "cure" will be short-lived.

A sick body and mind can lead to a sick spirit. A sick mind can produce a sick body.

How to dispel hopelessness?

Through belief in life's meaning.

Why believe in life's meaning when evil, suffering, and death exist?

Because Christ is risen.

How do we know this?

Believe, and you will see.

Nature is innocent and free. To be in touch with nature is to grow in freedom and innocence. Nature is not conscious, however, and it is totally without compassion. These are potentialities you must choose to develop to become truly human. Nature will not instill them in you.

CHANGING YOUR BEHAVIOR

On a separate sheet of paper or in a personal journal write your answers to the following questions. These questions will help you direct your efforts to change your behavior.

1. What addiction or False Self behavior have you identified that you would like to change? Choose only one to begin, then take another later.
2. Why would you like to change this behavior? What will happen if you do not change it?
3. What need or needs have you been trying to meet or cover up by using this behavior?

4. What are some other ways to meet these needs or to face the problems you are avoiding?

> *If you're out of touch with your thoughts and feelings, and experience a kind of tension and resistance to acknowledging limitations, there is probably a "should" blocking your awareness, attempting to force you into a role while filtering out all that does not fit that role. Drop it! Adults do not need "shoulds." Roles defined by "shoulds" kill the spirit. Only in authenticity and freedom can happiness be found.*

4

CENTERING
YOUR LIFE
IN GOD'S CARE

———

It really doesn't matter *what* you are doing (so long as it is not sin). It is *how* you do something that matters. In every moment, there is God. To do what you are doing in union with God: This is happiness.

we have noted that God is the center of the True Self. This is not to say that the True Self is God—only that the True Self cannot be known until our lives are centered in God. The discovery of God, then, enables the discovery of the True Self, and the discovery of the True Self reveals our centeredness in God. How, then, do we center our life in God?

First, we must see what kinds of false centers we have been living out of and how this has affected ourselves and others.

We may, of course, begin to work toward centering our life in God before we have thoroughly unmasked the False Self, but it is doubtful that we will get very far until we have done some of this work. If we avoid facing our False Self, it will talk us out of the spiritual journey as soon as we get tired. In fact, *the False Self is "that" within us which would have us not center our lives in God.* Noticing how this works is a good way to see how the False Self operates.

Next, we must ask ourselves, *Who is this God and what would it mean to be centered in God?* These questions put us in touch with our images of God and our ideas about what it means to be a Christian. They address the intellectual dimension of our faith response, and this is very important. Without intellectual conviction, the will has no focus or direction.

Finally, we must decide if we will make God the most important person in our life. If our answer to this is "yes," we will discover that prayer is no longer an option for us but a way of nourishing the deepest hungers of our heart.

DISCOVERING YOUR IMAGES OF GOD

Listed below are a few suggestions for discovering how your images of God affect your willingness to center your life in God.

1. What words and/or symbols describe how you understood God when you were a young child? How did these affect your willingness to be close to God? (After responding to these questions about your childhood, consider your adolescent years, young adult years, and other times in life up to your present situation.)

2. The New Testament teaches that Jesus Christ is the visible manifestation of the invisible God. (See Col 1:15.) In other

words, Jesus Christ is the true image of God. If you want to know what God is like, look to Jesus. If you do not know much about Jesus, read the Gospels and make notes on what Jesus suggests to you about the true nature of God (especially in his parables).

    a. What does Jesus reveal to you about the nature of God?
    b. What does Jesus reveal to you about God's attitude toward human beings?
    c. How are Jesus' revelations about God like or unlike your own images of God discovered in question one on the preceding page?

3. Ask your spiritual director or a mature Christian to recommend books that can help you grow to a healthy understanding of God.

If you stand before God, another, and/or creation wanting to "get" something, you will be anxious and unfree. If you stand willing to love, accepting in gratitude what is given, you will be peaceful and free.

BELONGING TO GOD

In baptism, you have been claimed by the Church for Christ. Your soul has been grafted into his Mystical Body and so shares in the Life of the Body. But the False Self system is capable of rejecting this Life. In Christian spirituality, we strive to live out the meaning of our baptism through a life of faith and love. The following reflections can help you grow in this faith. As you consider the questions following each statement, you may want to note your thoughts and responses on a separate sheet of paper or in a personal journal.

1. In a very real sense, your life is most influenced by what you think is most important. What you think most important, you belong to.

   a. What or who has been most important in your life through the years?
   b. How has this affected your sense of who you are?

2. Christ wants you to belong to him above all. (See Mt 12:46–50; 13:44–46; 16:24–25; 10:34–39; Lk 18:18–25, and many others.)

   a. To what extent do you experience yourself as belonging to Christ?
   b. How do you feel about belonging to Christ above all else?
   c. What are some of your fears about belonging to Christ?
   d. What attracts you to a commitment of belonging to Christ?

3. To belong to Christ is to entrust your life to his care. This entrusting is what is meant by *faith*.

   a. How have your erroneous images of God affected your willingness to entrust your life to God's care?
   b. Is Jesus Christ a person whom you think you can trust? Why or why not?
   c. Are you willing to entrust your life to the care of Christ? This is the decision of faith.

WALKING WITH CHRIST

What would it mean to entrust your life to the care of Jesus Christ? Do you just sit back and let him do everything for you, or is there something you must do? This exercise focuses on these questions by reflecting on the gospel image of being yoked with Jesus: "Come to me, all you that are weary and are carrying heavy burdens, and I will give you rest. Take my yoke upon you, and learn from me, for I am gentle and humble in heart, and you will find rest for your souls. For my yoke is easy, and my burden is light" (Mt 11:28–30). As you consider the following questions, keep in mind these two images regarding the yoke: (1) Two pulling together, Christ and you; if you do not walk, the yoke will not go forward; (2) If you walk too fast or in the wrong direction, Christ will resist this. You may want to note your responses to these questions on a separate sheet of paper or in a personal journal.

1. What are the signs that you are living too fast or too slowly?
2. How do you know when your life is going in the wrong direction?
3. Christ provides the gifts of direction and pace. How do you experience Christ doing this in your life?
4. What are some ways in which you and other people try to get God to do for you what you must do for yourself?
5. What can God do in you and for you that you cannot do for yourself?

The yoke image tells you that you must walk—that Christ cannot walk for you, only with you.

A PRAYERFUL CELEBRATION OF ENTRUSTING AND COMMITMENT

This is a short, powerful way to entrust your life to God's care. Use it frequently.

Opening prayer

> God, I abandon myself into your hands;
>   do with me what you will.
> Whatever you may do, I thank you:
> I am ready for all; I accept all
> and in all your creatures—
> I wish no more than this, O God.
> Into your hands I commend my soul;
> I offer it to you with all my heart,
> for I love you, God,
> and so need to give myself,
> to surrender myself into your hands without reserve
>   and with boundless confidence,
>   for you are my God.
>
> *Charles de Foucauld*

Affirmation

> God can and will do in me and for me what I could never do for myself.

Commitment

> I, for my part, must be willing to use my own human powers in the service of honesty, love, peace. Toward these ends, I am willing

- to claim my will to live because I exist; I will not indulge depressing, life-negating thoughts or feelings
- to love myself because I am alive—because God wills my existence
- to discover and cherish my giftedness, even if others disapprove of my doing so
- to learn healthy, loving ways to meet my needs
- to trust in the loving providence of God concerning the future
- to pray for God's help and to call another person when I feel like indulging my addictive fix
- to keep my attention focused in love all through the day

Closing prayer

The LORD is my light and my salvation;
    whom shall I fear?
The LORD is the stronghold of my life;
    of whom shall I be afraid?

Though an army encamp against me,
    my heart does not fear;
though war rise up against me,
    yet I will be confident.
One thing I asked of the LORD,
    that will I seek after:
to live in the house of the LORD
    all the days of my life,
to behold the beauty of the LORD
    and to inquire in his temple.
Psalm 27:1,3–4

To know the better way and to refuse to follow it: This is a choice for sin and building up of the False Self.

THE HOLY SPIRIT

The Holy Spirit is the third Person of the Trinity, who is also one with the Father and the Son. The gift of the Holy Spirit enabled the apostles to move from sorrow and grief to courage and joy. Without the Holy Spirit, we are left to ourselves, trying to imitate and follow Jesus but lacking the will and resolve to do so. We need the Holy Spirit to live the Christian life; without the Holy Spirit, it is impossible to remain centered in God.

With the sacraments of baptism and confirmation, a Christian is blessed with the gift of the Holy Spirit. As with any of God's gifts, however, the Spirit can be neglected to such an extent that we do not even notice the effects in our lives.

To open to the gift of the Holy Spirit, we need only ask. (See Lk 11:13.) When we ask for the gift of the Spirit to enable us to know God's will and to act accordingly, we may be sure that our prayer is answered.

The presence of the Holy Spirit is experienced in many ways:

- as a firm inner resolve to live for Christ
- as a gentle guidance in our thinking process
- as an inner Presence of sweetness, peace, and joy
- as a firm inner opposition to wrongdoing
- as the Source of our desire to pray—especially in praise

Pray often to the Holy Spirit! We need not use a special prayer, although many such prayers exist. We ask in our own words for the Spirit to manifest as described previously. We ask throughout the day, and learn to live in the guidance of the Spirit.

*I*f one thing still seems better than
another, one moment more full of life
than another, one moment better than
another—you are still immature. God
saturates all moments and all things.
To experience this is the end of desiring
and preferring. Serenity!

THE GIFTS OF THE HOLY SPIRIT

Traditional Catholic spirituality has viewed spiritual growth in terms of an increase in the gifts of the Holy Spirit. These gifts are graces that enable the individual to live a holy life; indeed, they are a perfect description of holiness. They are obtained through prayer and sacrament but sustained through living a life of love and service, which the gifts make possible.

The Infused Gifts (ISA 11:2, 3)

The infused gifts are truly gifts—presents of the Holy Spirit who freely gives the responsive soul powerful abilities: four endowments of the intellect (wisdom, understanding, knowledge, and counsel) and three emotion-related gifts (piety, fortitude, and fear of God).

1. *Wisdom:* The integration of divine truth into everyday life
2. *Understanding:* The ability of the Soul to grasp divine truth

3. *Knowledge:* Ability to judge things in the light of faith
4. *Counsel:* Ability to discern well and make good decisions
5. *Piety:* Produces a love of God
6. *Fortitude:* The courage and strength of will to live according to God's plan
7. *Fear of God:* Profound respect for the justice and majesty of God

The Charismatic Gifts
(from 1 Corinthians 12 and other sources)

The charismatic gifts are considered preternatural gifts in that they are manifestations of extrasensory powers under the guidance of the Holy Spirit for the building up of the Church. As such, these gifts do not indicate any special quality of holiness (as do the infused gifts), but they can be helps to holiness.

1. *Prophecy:* To hear a message from God and speak it
2. *Healing:* To communicate healing power to another in need
3. *Knowledge:* To know the secret thoughts, memories, feelings, or desires of another
4. *Visionaries:* To know the future or what's going on in another place at this time
5. *Inspired preaching:* To expound on God's Word in such a manner as to deeply inspire and motivate others
6. *Glossolalia:* To speak in an unknown language for purposes of giving praise to God or as a prelude to prophecy

In addition to the infused gifts of the Spirit, mystical theology has listed various fruits of the Holy Spirit as evidence of spiritual growth. These are mentioned in Galatians 5:22–23, where they are contrasted with the fruits of self-indulgence. The fruits of the Holy Spirit are *love, joy, peace, patience, kindness, generosity, faithfulness, gentleness, and self-control.*

*N*o need to "guard" your experiences
of God and true life. That which guards
and tries to perpetrate it is the obstacle
to its ongoing realization.

THE EUCHARIST

The Christian plan is for the sick and weakened human Soul to be joined with the divine/human person of Christ and so to be strengthened to live as God has intended for it to live. We are not saved by "doing the right things" or through spiritual disciplines, but by virtue of our union with the living and risen Christ.

Union with Christ begins with baptism and deepens through living a life of faith, hope, and love. Our union with him is a gift, not something we earn; on our own, there is absolutely nothing we can do to attain union with him. That we meet him in prayer and through faith are due to his generosity, not to our deservingness.

When Jesus ascended to the right hand of the Father, he did not go away: he disappeared! This means that he no longer manifested in a localized, physical human form to only a small group but became present to the whole universe through the realm of the Spirit. It is through this realm that he continues to come to us, especially through the gift of the Eucharist.

At every Mass, Christ is manifest in and through the gathered assembly, the Scriptures, the priest, and the consecrated bread and wine. We need to allow ourselves to be nourished in all these ways.

In receiving the consecrated bread and wine, we receive the body and blood of Christ and are joined in the Word most intimately with our priest and our community to his invisible, living Body of Christ. When we eat regular food, it becomes part of our human body; when we consume the body and blood of Christ, we become part of his Body.

The gift of the Eucharist is Christ feeding his Church. We need this food and we need it often. The Church recommends that all Catholics be nourished by Eucharist at least once a week. This is a minimal requirement. More frequent participation in Mass and reception of the Eucharist is strongly encouraged if we wish to grow closer to Christ.

> *Faith comes not from intellectual conviction, but from an open, trusting "yes" to God's invitation to loving unity. Of course, without intellectual conviction, the mind will not instruct the will to say "yes." Even so, faith opens one to realms that the mind cannot know.*

THE BASICS OF PERSONAL PRAYER

Just as two lovers cannot grow closer without taking special time to talk to each other and be together, so it is with us and Christ. This is why personal prayer is so important. As Saint Alphonsus so beautifully put it, "Prayer is talking and listening to God about the things that pertain to our friendship."

Prayer is so obviously necessary for growth in Christ. Why are so few Christians really committed to spending time with God daily? The answer again is the False Self system. Prayer spells death to the False Self, and the False Self exists to control our lives according to its own fearful values. Prayer, on the other hand, invites God to direct our lives. We can see how the False Self would perceive this as a conflict.

All the excuses people use to avoid daily prayer come from the False Self—and not one of those excuses has any real validity! It may be, for example, that there are mornings when we don't have time because the alarm clock fails to ring or a small child's needs take precedence. But these are exceptional situations. Everyone has plenty of time for prayer. If nothing else, we can get up earlier to pray, for sleep lost due to prayer will not be missed.

A first consideration for growing in prayer, then, is that we must make a *commitment of time* to be with God daily. I recommend a minimum of twenty to thirty minutes. It takes that long just to quiet down and listen. If possible, choose a time of the day when you are awake and energetic. (Bringing to God your leftover psychic energy at the end of the day might be the best you can do, but how would you like it if your lover did this to you on a regular basis?) Getting started is the hard part, and the False Self will put up a great resistance. After a few weeks, though, you will wonder how you ever lived without prayer. (If you are already taking this time, you know very well what I mean.)

Personal prayer time is to be spent in a context *of silence* and *solitude*. Communal prayer is very good, but it is no substitute for one-on-one time with God. You would not talk to your lover only in a crowd, would you? So, too, with God. Find a place where you can be alone and undisturbed. Ask your family to leave you in peace during your prayer time; they will benefit from the more peaceful and joyful attitude you bring to them. Ask them to take a message if you receive a phone call.

How do you spend this time with God? You may do whatever you wish, of course, and God will bless you for it. But to really enter into a sharing or dialogue with God, a simple format such as the one described below works well for most people.

1. *Quieting.* Take a few moments to come into the present. Notice the sounds around you, the feel of your clothing, your breathing. Ask the Holy Spirit to guide you in this time.

2. *Listening.* Slowly read a short passage of Scripture. Sometimes reading it aloud helps bring it to life. The passage you select should be something that provides food for thought. (You wouldn't want a genealogy, for example.) New Testament passages are strongly recommended—especially the gospel readings used for daily Mass. After reading the passage once, read it again, even more slowly, letting the message sink in. Here is a message to you from God.

3. *Meditation.* In Christianity, meditation means using your mind to consider the meaning of a sacred reading. If the reading touches off a spontaneous meditation, stay with it. This might mean sharing with God what you think and feel about what you have read. You might also want to use your imagination to meditate. For example, try to see Jesus standing before you, speaking the words of Scripture. There are many meditation books that can help you break open the Word of God. (See Suggested Reading, pages 147 to 148.)

4. *Affective Prayer.* After listening to the Word and considering its meaning to you, pray for the grace to carry out its message this day. You might be moved to pray for others, to thank God for favors received, or to express sorrow for shortcomings. This kind of prayer may come before listening and meditating if you are experiencing many feelings and preoccupations. Lift them up to the Lord first, and then you will have a quiet place within to listen.

5. *Silent adoration.* It is good to just "be" with God in silence and love. Sometimes this will be easy for you—a natural and spontaneous outgrowth of your dialogue with God. Regardless, simply be silent before God during the

final five to ten minutes of prayer. If you begin to practice centering prayer (see pages 136 to 137), you may wish to be silent even longer. You might envision God as an invisible, loving Light and feel yourself being silently energized by this Light. You might also use a simple word or short phrase ("Praise you, Lord God" or "My Lord and my God") to bring your attention to God in silence.

As the months and years go by, you will find yourself being drawn more and more to silent forms of prayer. This resting in God in loving silence is called *contemplative prayer*. Even advanced contemplatives, however, recommend beginning with a short period of listening and meditating before letting themselves plunge into the deep Silence. Listening and meditating prepare the mind for this Silence and enable you to rest there in peace and stability.

> W*ithout love, the Light of consciousness fades, so that consciousness is just a computer spinning out programs to solve problems it has created for itself.*

TRUE PRAYER

In all my prayers, I shall remember

1. That I am a creature, a contingent being, entirely dependent on God for my existence
2. That there is nowhere to go and nothing to do to be happy. There is only to do "whatever," pleasant or unpleasant, in union with God. Practically speaking, this means to do what I am doing and nothing else—to do it with an open heart and nonjudgmental mind.

3. That my own ascetical practices apart from love of God make me more self-righteous and less open to intimacy
4. That God is an undefinable Mystery
5. That my intent in prayer needs to be affirming of God as Creator, and inviting the Spirit to work in my soul to make me a Christ. A short, simple "Yes, Lord," spoken not with the lips but in the silence of the heart, may summarize all of the above.
6. The purpose of prayer, then, is to become entrained in this manner of living. In prayer, all preconceptions, good ideas, and projections are encountered in the silence. I see them and let them go. To simply breathe in God's love, open in all levels of being, letting God form me, submitting any self-movement to the Spirit—that is entrainment for happiness.

The stream knows where it is going,
and the raft of Christ will hold.
Stay on board. Trust! Have fun!

SPIRITUAL DIRECTION: COMPANION ON THE SPIRITUAL JOURNEY

It is helpful to have a companion with whom we can share our joys and struggles in living the Christian life. This companion may be our spouse, another family member, or a close friend.

When we speak of spiritual direction, however, we are referring to a relationship that is more specifically focused on helping us live in faith. A spiritual director listens and gives feedback about what he or she is hearing and sensing about the movement of the Holy Spirit in our life. This feedback is for our consideration only; the spiritual director is not a guru who tells us what to do.

The ideal of spiritual direction is soundly rooted in our understanding of Christian community. The Christian journey is not meant to be an individualistic, privatized spirituality. It is in community that we discover who we are and what we have to share. Spiritual direction provides an opportunity for a friendly and discerning experience of Christian community. As a community of two, my spiritual director and I attempt to discern what the Spirit is doing in my life and how I am being called to share my giftedness.

From the foregoing, it should already be obvious that spiritual direction is fundamentally different from psychotherapy. A counselor is not concerned with our spiritual center nor with how the Holy Spirit is leading us. The goals of psychotherapy are to help us deal with painful emotions and to support us in making difficult choices about relationships.

A spiritual director may deal with the same issues, of course, but from a different perspective. Painful feelings may be discussed in terms of how they lead away from God or toward God. Difficult relationships are reviewed to discern how God is calling us to love other people and ourselves as well.

Because spiritual direction and psychotherapy have different goals and emphases, it is possible to benefit from both at the same time. A person should not refrain from spiritual direction because he or she is in counseling. Nor should anyone choose a spiritual director over a counselor. In fact, spiritual directors who guide people away from psychotherapy are doing their directees a disservice.

It sometimes happens that a spiritual director is also a trained counselor. Even so, the director and directee need to be clear about what precisely is going on in their work together.

Finally, we note that psychotherapists generally meet with their clients once a week or more. Such frequent meetings are necessary to process the many feelings and attitudinal changes going on in the person's life. Spiritual directors, on the other hand, seldom meet with directees more than once every two weeks in the beginning of the relationship. After a while, once a month is usually sufficient.

> *Don't know how to love God?*
> *Very well, love people and creations,*
> *and that will be enough.*

HOW SPIRITUAL DIRECTION WORKS

As you consider spiritual direction and the possibility of a retreat, you will need to know the following basic information.

The agenda in spiritual direction: Some spiritual directors have a set agenda for time spent with their directees; most do not. You will usually be allowed to talk about anything you have on your mind. If your sharing seems to have nothing to do with living the Christian life, the director will eventually try to steer the discussion in that direction by asking how what you have shared is affecting your prayer life or your relationship with God.

The first few meetings usually are spent just getting to know each other. The director will want to know all about your life. Telling your story to another in this way will help you come to know yourself better; the listening presence of the director is also a source of great healing. Because the spiritual director is not in the same role as a counselor, he or she may also choose to tell you much about his or her life and faith journey. This can help you see the director as a fellow pilgrim on the journey rather than as a guru with all the answers.

After getting to know each other, you and the director may decide on a few structured activities to work on (such as those in this book), or you may agree to go through a book on spiritual growth together. Many directors are trained in the Spiritual Exercises of Saint Ignatius and use these in some manner with their directees. I like to use the Twelve Steps with people I work with. Some directors know a great deal about keeping a personal journal and may encourage you to keep one if you haven't already started doing so. Most directors these days also respect the fact that different human temperaments are drawn in different ways by the Spirit, so they might want to help you discover your personality type.

As you can see, many kinds of issues can be discussed in spiritual direction. Of paramount importance, however, is your life of prayer. A spiritual director is one who will hold you accountable for daily prayer. He or she will be interested in hearing what is happening during your prayer and will help you deepen your growth in prayer.

Choosing a spiritual director: We have already noted that a spiritual director is not a guru who will tell you what to do and what not to do. I would also like to make a distinction between a spiritual director and a sponsor in a Twelve Step program. A sponsor is one who has been in such a program for some time and can help new arrivals learn how to recover from addictive involvements by using the Twelve Steps. This is a form of spiritual companionship, to be sure, but I recommend that your spiritual director be more than just a "big buddy" for the spiritual journey.

Ideally, your spiritual director should be a person with some formal training or experience in this area. He or she should have knowledge of the Catholic mystical tradition and should be at least generally familiar with psychological development. Your director should be a person of prayer who has attended one or more eight-day silent directed retreats. Finally, he or she should also be in spiritual direction with another and should have already worked through painful issues from the past.

I consider these minimal requirements for a Catholic spiritual director. Not many meet these requirements, but there are enough who do. Generally, the ministry staff at a retreat center is a good resource for finding a spiritual director. Most religious communities also have a few qualified people. Some diocesan priests meet the minimal requirements, and more laypeople than ever are functioning effectively in this role.

If you do not already have a spiritual director and don't know whom to ask, I suggest you call your local retreat house. If you know of no such center, ask your parish priest for advice. Even after choosing someone, do not think you have to stay with that person. Agree with your director to give the relationship a trial for a while. Then, after a few sessions, evaluate whether you feel comfortable enough to continue.

Fees: It is typical for Christians to view ministry as something they have already paid for in the Sunday collection. This holds true for many parish services, but that is the limit.

Spiritual direction is really a professional service; therefore, be prepared to offer compensation to your director—especially if he or she is not an employee of the parish to which you tithe. Typically, the director will suggest that you make a donation to his or her retreat center or religious community. Some directors are self-employed; in this case, your compensation would be given directly to the individual.

Seldom does a director have a set fee such as psychotherapists do, and you would probably never be refused for non-payment. Nevertheless, I recommend a minimum donation of fifteen dollars per session. If this is more than you can afford, give what you can—even if it is a batch of cookies or a handwritten thank-you note. You will feel better for giving something in return for this service, and your director will appreciate it, too.

*A*ttention is a light that energizes. What
you attend to, you energize. Beware! If you
attend too long to temptation, it shall come
to pass. If you keep your mind fixed on
being here/now/in-love-to-love, you will
always be happy.

ON MAKING A RETREAT

Spiritual directors often suggest that their directees consider
making a retreat. Even if your own spiritual director doesn't
make this suggestion, it is an idea worth serious consideration.
After all, life is busy and noisy and, if we are not careful, we
will lose touch with ourselves and fall prey to fragmentation
and dissipation. To remain whole and "in touch," we need to
take time each day to let go of our busy-ness and be still with
God. We also need to "keep holy the Sabbath," which is why
the Church forbids any unnecessary servile work on Sundays.
On the positive side, we can go to Mass, visit our families, and
"laze around." In a culture that ultimately traces the value of
everything to dollars and cents, this taking time each day for
prayer and giving our Sundays to the Lord is a most counter-
cultural stance.

Making a retreat takes this stance a step further. On a retreat we commit several (or many) days to focusing attention
to our spiritual life. We leave our ordinary everyday environments and go off to another place to focus on our relationship
with God. We have our precedent for doing this in the example of Jesus and his disciples. (See Mk 6:31.) Things are no
different now than they were then except that now, *we* are the
disciples and he calls *us* to leave our busy-ness behind for a
while to spend time with him.

Types of retreats: But what exactly is a retreat? What goes on there? Twenty years ago these questions would have been easy to answer. At that time there were basically two types of retreats, silent-directed retreats and silent-preached retreats. The latter also included times for the rosary, the Way of the Cross, and other devotionals.

Glancing through the offerings of retreat centers today, however, we find many additional possibilities. (Many centers no longer offer silent-directed or silent-preached retreats.) Many creative and effective models for retreats have been developed and popularized during the past twenty years. As a result of this virtual explosion in retreat innovation, more choices are available. If we wish to "come away and rest for a while," there are many ways to do so. The type of retreat we choose to attend will depend largely on what we perceive our needs to be at a particular time in our life.

Here are some broad, general categories of retreats:

- *Directed:* A directed retreat will usually be from three to thirty days, using the Spiritual Exercises of Saint Ignatius of Loyola. Silence is observed, except during Mass and the daily meeting with the director. Three to five prayer periods a day are recommended.
- *Private:* In a private retreat, you simply pay room and board to a retreat center, using the time and place to "get away from it all." You design your own schedule for prayer and silence and plug into the center's schedule for Mass and meals.
- *Preached:* The usual time span for a preached retreat is three to five days, with two preached conferences each day, generally developing a theme through the retreat. Between conferences, there may be times for silence, Mass, individual sessions of spiritual direction, and unstructured "free" times. Traditional for-

mats will also include times for praying the rosary, the Way of the Cross, and other devotionals.

- *Guided:* This type of retreat usually lasts three to eight days, with one preached conference per day, individual sessions, and silence.
- *Group dynamic:* This retreat format is usually offered over a weekend and includes several talks, times for discussion, group activities, Eucharist, and reconciliation. The awakening of faith in the context of community is emphasized. Cursillo, Marriage Encounter, Engaged Encounter, Beginning Experience, Teens Encounter Christ, Awakening, Search, Parish Renewal, and other popular retreat programs are examples of this format.
- *Charismatic:* Times for teaching, praise, fellowship, and Mass, generally in a large-group context, characterize charismatic retreats. Their distinctive feature is the emphasis on praise and the manifestation of the gifts of the Spirit in building community. These are usually weekend-long retreats.
- *Contemplative:* A contemplative retreat will last from three to ten days, usually including brief periods of teaching or instruction, individual sessions for spiritual direction, and several periods a day for sitting quietly in God's loving presence. Retreats on centering prayer and Zen retreats belong to this type.
- *Twelve Steps:* This type of retreat is a combination of the preached and group dynamic formats, usually held over a weekend. In addition to conferences, there is time for Twelve Step meetings.
- *Specialty:* Some retreats may fit none of the above categories. Instead, they develop a specific theme using teachings, quiet periods, worksheets, group discussion, and other dynamics. Retreats on the Myers-

Briggs personality tool, the Enneagram, healing the child within, journaling, male spirituality, female spirituality, yoga, creation spirituality, wellness, and many other topics can be found in the offerings of retreat centers today. These may last from a weekend to a week, and usually feature speakers with expertise in the theme being emphasized.

What kind of retreat is right for you? Ideally, this is a question that your spiritual director/companion could help you answer. If you have no such help in your life, I encourage you to find someone. In the meantime, the best way to decide is to read through the offerings of retreat centers in your area and see what interests you. If you feel moved to attend a particular retreat, ask the Holy Spirit to confirm this for you in some manner—maybe by simply giving you the conviction that this is what you need at this time in your life. Generally, the retreats that look interesting to you will be retreats that address some of your needs.

Once you make your decision, you must register with the center. I mention this obvious fact because too often people put this off until the last minute only to discover to their disappointment that the retreat has been "filled." So get out your checkbook and register as soon as you know what you want to do. It is impossible to register too early for a retreat.

Make the most of it: If I could recommend one thing to people, it would be that *you be open to what the Lord wants to tell you or show you during the retreat.* We spend much of our time telling God, ourselves, and other people who we think we are. On a retreat it is time to listen to what God has to say about who you are.

A retreat is a special and blessed time. If you are open to the retreat process, the Lord can accomplish more with you during even a relatively brief retreat than during months of ordinary, everyday growth. I have experienced this time and again myself and have talked with others who have had the same experience in retreats through the years.

Frequently, expectations people bring to the retreat prevent this experience from happening. Many come expecting a certain "thing" to happen to them, and they refuse to let go of this expectation, even when it becomes clear that God has something else in mind. In other words, your own preconceptions about what *should* be happening to you on retreat often place obstacles in the way of your receiving fully what God has to offer you.

No doubt, however, you will spend some time telling God how you think and feel about things during the retreat. While some retreat formats encourage this, they all encourage you to *listen* to what God has to say to you. This listening may come through Scripture, a talk, a memory, a journal exercise—there are many ways it can happen. If you are open to it and praying for it, God will let you know this during the retreat. Such knowledge is worth every penny you invest in the retreat and every bit of pain you experience in coming to the knowledge. For, in the end, who we really are has nothing to do with our own ideas but with God's view of us. And *God's* view, we learn, is generally more honest, loving, and freeing than our own.

It is this kind of knowledge that a retreat invites us to experience. It is this kind knowledge that we truly hunger for.

> G *od cannot be experienced through our efforts, meditations, and ascetical techniques. The most we can do is come to receptive silence. Whatever God reveals is up to God.*

5

RECONCILIATION AND INNER TRANSFORMATION

———

When you interact with others in a manner unto growth and fun, God moves among and through you, enriching the human bond. When you refuse to interact with others in this manner, you become a "knot," blocking the flow of God in the human community.

it has been said that the love of God is "obtained" through faith, prayer, and sacrament but "retained" through the love of neighbor. Another saying has it that "you can't give what you don't have, but you can't keep what you don't share." These are important spiritual principles.

Our spiritual journey is concerned with cultivating a personal relationship with God through Christ. This is according to the will of Christ, who said, "Come to me, all you that are weary and are carrying heavy burdens, and I will give you rest" (Mt 11:28). Jesus wants us to share in his own special love-bond (the Holy Spirit) with the Father and to grow in that love. This is the new life that will go on forever.

Spiritual growth, as already mentioned, is not to be a private matter. We cannot grow in the love of God without growing in the love of ourselves and other people. "Those who say, 'I love God,' and hate their brothers or sisters, are liars" (1 Jn 4:20). Indeed, it seems that the love of God that comes through faith, prayer, and sacrament is directly related to our love of neighbor. In the Lord's Prayer we learn that God will forgive us our trespasses as we forgive others. In another place, we hear Jesus saying that reconciliation with our neighbor is a prerequisite for authentic prayer and worship. (See Mt 5:23–24.) God will not allow us to use his love as a drug with which to escape our responsibility to build a healthy human community.

This chapter presents resources to help you examine your human relationships, to make amends where necessary, and to forgive those who have wronged you. Not only are these things important for ongoing spiritual growth, the False Self feeds upon the guilt, fear, shame, resentment, and hurt resulting from troubled relationships. These painful emotional energies pull you away from your true center and influence you to adopt a defensive, controlling posture toward others. If you are to grow spiritually, you will need to diminish the power of the False Self in your consciousness, and one of the best ways to do this is to starve it to death by depriving it of emotional pain. Forgiveness and reconciliation are ways to obtain this healing.

RENEWAL OF MIND

In addition to the healing of emotions, a healing of attitudes is also called for. Reconciling with others will do us no good if we persist in old habits of judging, criticizing, and blaming ourselves and others for things that are relatively unimportant. To grow spiritually, we must "be transformed by the renewing of your minds, so that you may discern what is the will of God—what is good and acceptable and perfect" (Rom 12:2). In addition, "to put away your former way of life, corrupt and deluded by its lusts, and to be renewed in the spirit of your minds, and to clothe yourselves with the new self, created according to the likeness of God in true righteousness and holiness" (Eph 4:22–24). If we do not change our habits of thinking and judging, the False Self system will continue to create misery for us and project ill-will in all our relationships.

Many unhealthy attitudes are changed through prayer and meditation. Even so, ongoing vigilance is necessary. We must learn to detect negative and judgmental thoughts as soon as they begin and redirect our thinking in a more rational and loving direction. This is unquestionably the most difficult work of all in the process of spiritual transformation. Old, negative habits of thinking and judging can be so deeply ingrained that they function automatically and reactively without our permission—even against our will. "For I do not do the good I want, but the evil I do not want is what I do. Now if I do what I do not want, it is no longer I that do it, but sin that dwells within me" (Rom 7:19–20).

Through our ongoing efforts to live a spiritual life, we come to recognize in ourselves another will or energy that stands in opposition to the automatic, judgmental reactions of the False Self. The encounter between this spiritual will and the False Self system is nothing short of an inner civil war. Many people turn back when this war begins. As noted earlier, it is a most difficult time on the journey. But to turn back is only to guarantee victory for the False Self system. There is nothing to do but to live through the civil war, knowing that its turbulent commotion is a good sign that inner transformation is taking place.

In the meantime, we can do a few things to help ourselves.

1. We can continue to be faithful through prayer, the Eucharist, and reconciliation with others.
2. We can rejoice that this civil war is taking place within us, rather than running away from it. In time the war will end, for the victory has already been won by Christ.
3. Inner transformation is a time when spiritual direction is especially helpful; we need this support to carry on.
4. Finally, we can practice affirmations that help implant deep within us a healthier system of thoughts and judgments. A few suggestions toward this end are provided in the following sections.

You are not alone in caring for your growth. You are responsible, but there is much help available: Christ, the angels, saints, and the Church on earth are here to help you. They want to help you. Let them.

EXAMEN OF CURRENT RELATIONSHIPS

On a separate sheet of paper or in a personal journal, write the name of a person with whom you are in relationship, and record your answers to the following questions.

1. What do I and this person do together or have in common?
2. How would I describe the bond that exists between us, intellectually, emotionally, and spiritually?
3. What qualities of character do I admire in this person?
4. Which of this person's behaviors do I most appreciate? (Resolve to tell him or her about which behaviors are hard for you to accept. How do you feel about each of these behaviors?)
5. What could *I* do more of and less of to improve this relationship? (Be specific and use statements such as "more of..." or "less of...")
6. What would I like the *other person* to *do* more of and less of to help improve this relationship? (Be specific and use statements such as "more of..." or "less of..." Resolve to ask for these changes at some time in the future.)

*J*ust look and see from the heart.
No thoughts. No judgments.
Enlightenment! Indescribable bliss!

PREPARING FOR RECONCILIATION WITH OTHERS

Reconciling with other people requires preparation, and I can think of no better approach than step eight of the Twelve Steps: *Made a list of all persons we had harmed and became willing to make amends to them all.*

There are three key concepts in this statement.

1. *Made a list.* It is important to evaluate a relationship carefully before attempting some kind of reconciliation with the other person.

2. *All persons we had harmed.* We first need to see how our lives have affected others. After doing so, we may see how others have hurt us in some manner.
3. *Willing to make amends to them all.* This quality of willingness is absolutely necessary. Without it, we will not be able to release our hurts and resentments.

To prepare yourself for reconciliation with others, I suggest you review your relationship with one person at a time, responding to the following questions on a separate sheet of paper or in a personal journal:

1. What has a relationship with this person meant to me during the different times of my life?
2. What specific situations have contributed to problems between us?
3. How have I hurt this person by word, deed, or neglect?

   • How do I feel about each of these?
   • What have been the consequences to this person, to me, and to our relationship?

4. How has this person hurt or angered me by words, deeds, or neglect?

   • How do I feel about each of these?
   • What have been the consequences to this person, to me, and to our relationship?

These are obviously difficult questions to answer. If you have never reviewed your relationships before, I suggest that you take at least one good, hard look at them using this format. After going through this reflection and following through in the manner suggested in the next exercise, you will be more

free from painful emotions related to relationships. This freedom will enable you to maintain yourself in a stance of
centeredness in Christ.

You may find it helpful to share your reflections from this
exercise with your spiritual director before planning to take
any action. It helps to share these hurts with another, and your
spiritual director will accept you and listen to you no matter
what you have discovered about yourself. This can increase
both your willingness to make amends and your readiness to
do so.

*A triangle is a form that may be expressed
in an infinite number of ways. So, too, with
Christ: He is the human form, and each
person is a specific manifestation of what
it means to be Christ.*

RECONCILING WITH OTHERS

This exercise is a follow-up to the previous one, "Preparing for
Reconciliation With Others." It is based on step nine of the
Twelve Steps: *Made direct amends to such people whenever
possible, except when to do so would injure them or others.*

Having honestly evaluated your relationships in the spirit
of the eighth step, you must now decide what to do about
these relationships. Holding on to old hurts and resentments
hurls you much more than it hurts another, and yet the ninth
step points out the importance of using discretion in attempting reconciliation.

As in the previous exercise, we make a distinction here
between what you have done to others and what they have
done to you. In reconciling with others, you must make amends

for the harm you have done to them, and you must forgive them for the hurts they have caused you. Making amends and forgiving others are the two methods of reconciling with others. I suggest you consider them separately, although they are surely related.

For each relationship you examined in the previous exercise, consider the following questions:

1. What kinds of amends must I make?

   - *Apologize for specific behaviors:* Mention consequences: "I apologize for cursing at you when we argued last week. I know this hurt your feelings and that you felt embarrassed when your friends laughed about my remark. I've felt badly about this ever since." This kind of sharing may be done in direct personal communication, by phone, or in writing.
   - *Make restitution:* Repay money or repair damages done; return something gained from dishonest behavior. This, too, may be done in writing or through verbal communication.
   - *Do nothing:* If making amends will hurt the other person unnecessarily, it is better to do nothing. Your amends can be your ongoing efforts to be honest and loving.

2. How can I forgive this person?

   - *Communicate directly:* Tell the other person what he or she did or said that hurt or angered you. Discuss the behavior and how you felt; do not discuss motives, which you do not know. Finally, let the other person know that you forgive him or her. You may also ask for a change of behavior. For example, you might say, "Last week when you came home late without calling, I felt hurt and very angry that you didn't even acknowledge it when you finally did arrive. I have decided to forgive you for this. I will not mention it again, and I will let go of my anger about it, but I do ask that you call me the next time you will be late." Although this kind of communication works best if shared person to person, it may be better to write it to the other if you have trouble sharing feelings verbally.

- *Write a letter:* Write it, but do not mail it or share it with the other person. You may choose to share it with your spiritual director, however. This is often the best approach in relationships in which the other person is still too unhealthy to listen to you without harming you. It also works well in relationships with persons who have died. In the latter case, you may choose to read your letter at the grave site or in another, prayerful context.

After making your best efforts to forgive others and to make amends, you have done all that spirituality asks you to do to be at peace with your past. Let the past be. It is normal for emotions about the past to remain for some time after reconciliation, so you need not see this as a sign that you haven't forgiven (unless something new and important is presenting itself through your memory). Let the past be. Do not meddle in it any longer. In time, painful emotions about the past will fade.

A special word must be said about situations where people discover that they have been severely abused in the past. Forgiveness may not come easily in this case, and emotions may be turbulent. Do not hesitate to seek professional counseling to deal with these issues. Eventually, you must forgive those who have abused you if you are to be free within yourself, but

it may take the support of both spiritual direction and psychotherapy for you to do so.

> *L*ove is the only answer to all of your
> *"problems." Even when you are in deep*
> *mental anguish—the worst of all pains—*
> *love is the only answer. In loving, the Spirit*
> *configures your energies unto wholeness and*
> *serenity—eventually, that is, and not*
> *without suffering.*

DAILY EXAMEN

Many of the exercises presented in this book invite you to take
a long, hard look at your life. This is especially important if
you have never done so. But such comprehensive self-exami-
nation and reflection is not the norm for those living a spiritual life. They are major housecleanings, as it were. Once the
house is clean, you do not clean it all over again (unless you
are compulsive about such matters); you try to keep it clean,
which takes a little effort each day. Such a small daily inner
housecleaning is the *examen.*

Daily examen is usually done at the end of the day to look
back on the day and learn whatever lessons suggest themselves.
I recommend at least fifteen minutes for this, which can be
taken as a form of prayerful meditation or even a prayerful
walk before bedtime. The format below describes some of the
issues the examen ought to consider:

1. Begin with prayer to the Holy Spirit for guidance in looking back on your day.
2. If there is a strong feeling or issue on your mind, acknowl-

edge this and note its relevance to living a spiritual life. What is the Lord inviting you to do about this issue?

3. If there is no strong feeling—or after dealing with such an issue—slowly and prayerfully recall the events of your day as you experienced them. You need not dwell on any particular part of the day unless you discover strong or hidden feelings you had not noticed before, in which case you return to the approach suggested in the second point for dealing with such matters.

4. Having examined the events of your day, what have you earned?

   • When did you feel close to God?
   • When did you pull away from God? Ask for pardon.
   • What kind of growth do you note?
   • Do you need to forgive anyone or make amends? If so, resolve to do so as soon as possible.

5. Thank God for this day, and pray for a peaceful sleep.

Regular practice of the examen will help you to sleep well, for your mind will have come to rest before you go to bed. Consequently, your dreams will be more peaceful and you will wake up feeling refreshed.

The examen will help you grow in self-knowledge and will enable you to discover how you are living your spirituality each day. Using a journal for your examen can help you keep track of progress through the days and weeks as well as identify issues for discussion with your spiritual director or in the sacrament of reconciliation (penance).

As with many other things, the examen is a discipline. Along with prayer and frequent reception of the Eucharist, the examen is an indispensable tool for spiritual growth. If you practice it faithfully for a month, you will surely discover for yourself what I am talking about, and the discipline will become one that you look forward to.

THE SACRAMENT
OF RECONCILIATION

To help Christians live a spiritual life, the Catholic Church makes available the sacrament of reconciliation (also called the sacrament of penance). We recognize that there are times when our behavior proceeds from the False Self and this hurts other people and ourselves. When this happens, we must work toward reconciliation in our relationships.

But there is another dimension to this sinful behavior. Acting out of the False Self means that we have broken relationship with God and so have lost touch with our True Center. If we are to treat God as the most important person in our lives, we must be reconciled with God when we stray. This is the opportunity the sacrament of reconciliation extends to us.

This is not the place to discuss the proper way to prepare for the sacrament or to explain the rite itself. If you do not know how to do this, you can surely receive information and instruction from your local parish. Your reflections from the previous exercises (especially steps eight and nine and the daily examen) can be used as part of your sharing, but other matters should be considered as well—such as how you have been fulfilling your obligations to the Christian community.

The sacrament of reconciliation can help you honestly renew your commitment to God when you have seriously lost your way. Therefore, it is to be treated as an important resource for living a Christian spiritual life.

Sin is very pervasive. Its roots run very, very deep!

6

LIVING
IN THE SPIRIT

Love is not something we "should try
to do" over and against other impulses.
Love is who we are and what we do
when we are not concerned about
getting something for ourselves. To
live and act in this way is *the* meaning
of spirituality.

up to this point, the exercises in this book have focused
on helping you become established in your spiritual center and
grow in that life through prayer and healing. They have largely
emphasized your inner life to help you move from a life centered
in people and circumstances outside yourself (the centeredness
of the False Self) to a life centered in relationship with the
Spirit within.

But life cannot be spent looking inward. Through an ongoing life of prayer, with daily examen and frequent reception

of the Eucharist, you may trust that growth in your spiritual center will deepen and hold. The primary issues, then, move from concern about where you are centered to living in the Spirit all through the day.

Living constantly in the Spirit is not as easy as it may sound, however. Even those who have been living a spiritual life for years must still struggle with worldly temptations to pursue pleasure, popularity, wealth, and all the other addictions the False Self is prone to. You must also learn to meet your needs in a healthy manner. More than likely, you have learned to meet your basic needs in somewhat of a False Self mentality. We all have. Now, however, you must learn just what your real human needs are and what are mere wants and desires. This is where the influence of the world can confuse you. Here I will attempt to provide some direction in this area.

Discerning God's will is an issue that pertains to daily living. You have many gifts and talents—some of which you are already using in various ways, some of which you may not yet even recognize.

What is God calling you to do with these gifts and talents? A discerning response to this question enables you to remain centered in the Spirit all day long.

And then there is the issue of suffering. When the going gets rough, many abandon the spiritual journey. Sometimes it may happen that the pains you experience are directly related to your life in Christ—that if you were living a more worldly life, you wouldn't be experiencing rejection or inner conflict. These times are very important, for they are experiences of the cross of Christ. When you reject a cross, you fall back into the domain of the False Self. By learning to *carry* these crosses, you will experience a deepening of the love and fellowship of the Holy Spirit.

MEETING YOUR TRUE NEEDS

God has made us to be creatures with a wide variety of needs. In pursuing the fulfillment of these needs, human beings encounter one another and the creation. What is the nature of these encounters? And what kinds of needs are we attentive to? These are moral and spiritual issues no Christian can avoid facing.

As an adult and a Christian, you have the responsibility to meet your own needs. You cannot do this alone, of course, but neither should you expect that other people will take responsibility for knowing your needs and seeing to it that you care for yourself. Perhaps the best way to love yourself is to attend to your needs in healthy and responsible ways. In caring for yourself in this manner, you will be moved into contact with other human beings you can depend on for helping you meet your needs. Everyone is doing the same; this is how human community and culture are formed.

But what are your needs? How can you distinguish them from your wants?

These questions are not easy to answer. Generally, a *need* is considered to be a basic requirement for human health and wholeness; if you do not meet such a need, you are less healthy and whole. *Wants* are something altogether different and refer to the requirements of the False Self. Quite frequently, our wants are superimposed on our needs, such as when we purchase clothing for the purpose of being in style as well as for covering the body. Indeed, you will likely discover that the wants of the False Self have influenced the way you have been meeting your needs all along.

Living in the Spirit does not mean that you cease to have needs, only that you learn to meet them without giving in to the wants of the False Self.

For each of the needs listed below, consider the following four questions. You may want to record your responses on a separate sheet of paper or in a personal journal.

1. How have I met this need in the past?
2. How have the concerns of the False Self influenced the way I have met this need?
3. How could this need be met in a healthy and responsible manner, free from the wants of the False Self?
4. What, specifically, will I do to meet these needs in my life from now on?

Physical needs

- Food, water, and nutrition
- Exercise
- Sleep
- Shelter
- Clothing
- Medical care

Psychospiritual needs

- Play, fun, and humor
- Honest, caring relationships
- Sense of choice and freedom
- Sense of purpose, meaning, and hope
- Intellectual stimulation
- Aesthetic stimulation
- Prayer
- Creative expression

SHARING YOUR GIFTEDNESS

Each individual is unique. God has blessed you with gifts in a way that no one else is blessed. Your special gift may be something as simple as the ability to listen and empathize with others or as public as preaching the Good News. Whatever your gifts, it is certain that your ongoing spiritual growth will depend on your sharing them in some manner for the good of the Church. When you share your gifts, you are blessed, and this blessing brings a love of ministry.

The following questions are designed to help you discover your perception of your giftedness and how you are called to share yourself at this time in your life. You may want to record your responses to these questions on a separate sheet of paper or in a personal journal.

1. What kinds of gifts do I have to offer that may be of service to people?
2. How am I sharing these gifts at this time in my life?
3. Are there other gifts I think I might have?
4. What are some ways to develop my giftedness more fully?

Now, assume that money is no problem, and you can design your lifestyle any way you choose. Answer the following questions and give your reasons for each.

1. Would you be married, single, in a religious community?
2. If you are not married and would like to be, what qualities do you look for in a spouse? Would you like children to be part of your life?
3. Where would you like to live? What kind of home or living situation do you want?
4. What kind of work would you like to do?

5. How would you spend your time on a typical day?
6. How does answering these questions help you to actualize and express your giftedness?
7. How does the lifestyle you dream of reflect the values of your spiritual center?
8. If you are not already living this lifestyle, what stops you from doing so? What do you want to do about this obstacle to realizing your dreams?

Your life is your own, and Christ would have you live it and discover your way in honesty, questioning, and self-chosen surrender. He will teach and support.

DISCERNING GOD'S WILL

The following suggestions rely heavily on the guidelines for the discernment of spirits in the Spiritual Exercises of Saint Ignatius Loyola. They are to be used when attempting to discern God's will in major decisions about your life.

Theological assumptions relevant to discernment

1. God is a good God. God wants to give you much more than you want for yourself.
2. God knows who you are better than you know yourself. God also knows what you need in order to become the person he created; he knows this better than you know this about yourself.
3. When you are faced with a number of options, it is entirely possible that some are better for you than others, in terms of your overall human growth.

4. When you surrender your preferences for different options to God, you become free to discern God's preference (if any) among these options.

Principles for spiritual decision making

1. "When you are making a decision or choice, you are not deliberating about choices which involve sin (wrongdoing), but rather you are considering alternatives which are lawful and good" (Saint Ignatius).

2. It is not necessary to agonize over God's will in choosing between healthy options in the small affairs of everyday life. "Ordinarily there is nothing of such obvious importance in one rather than the other that there is need to go into long deliberation over it. You must proceed in good faith and without making subtle distinctions in such affairs and, as Saint Basil says, do freely what seems good to you so as not to weary your mind, waste your time, and put yourself in danger of disquiet, scruples, and superstitions" (Saint Francis de Sales).

3. In areas where you have binding commitments (such as marriage vows, parenting, religious vows), "your basic attitude should be that the only choice still called for is the full-hearted gift of self to this state of life" (Saint Ignatius). In other words, every effort must be made to live out the implications of your binding commitments, even if those commitments were poorly made. This does not mean, however, that you must suffer unnecessary abuse at the hands of another.

4. In areas of life where you have already made decisions that can be changed on the basis of what you had once discerned to be God's will, "your one desire should be to find your continued growth in the way of life you have chosen" (Saint Ignatius).

5. "If you have come to a poor decision in matters that are changeable, you should try to make a choice in the proper way, whether it would be maintaining the same pattern of life or it would demand a change" (Saint Ignatius).

6. If possible, you should avoid making important life decisions during times when you are emotionally upset, for it is likely that you would be running away from a problem rather than responding to God's call.

7. When attempting to discern among a number of options regarding significant lifestyle choices, you would do well to proceed as Saint Ignatius suggests in the following patterns:

First pattern

- Clearly place before your mind what it is you want to decide about. What are your options?
- Attempt to view each option with equal detachment, surrendering personal preferences to the care of God.
- Sincerely pray that God will enlighten and draw you in the direction leading to his praise and glory.
- List and weigh the advantages and disadvantages of the various dimensions of your proposed decision.
- Consider which alternative seems more reasonable. Then decide according to the more weighty motives and not from any selfish or sensual inclination.
- Having come to the decision, now turn to God again and ask him to accept and confirm it—if it is for his greater service and glory—by giving you a sense of serenity and holy conviction about this decision.

Second pattern

(This is an excellent follow-up on the first pattern to evaluate your decision from another angle.)

- Since the love of God should motivate your life, check yourself to see whether your attachment to the object of choice is solely because of your Creator and Lord.
- Imagine yourself in the presence of a person you have never met but who has sought your help in an attempt to respond better to God's call. Review what you would tell that person, and then observe the advice you would so readily give to another for whom you want the best.
- Ask yourself if at the moment of death you would make the same decision you are making now. Guide yourself by this insight, and make your present decision in conformity with it.
- See yourself standing before Christ your Judge when this life has ended and talking with him about the decision you have made at this moment in your life. Choose now the course of action you feel will give you happiness and joy in the presence of Christ on the Day of Judgment.

True understanding is impossible to attain conceptually. To attempt this is like trying to define the smell of a rose or the experience of falling in love. The heart knows love and truth far more clearly than the intellect.

GUIDELINES FOR HEALTHY RELATIONSHIPS

Use the following concepts to evaluate and monitor the health of your human relationships. You may wish to write your responses and comments in your journal.

1. If you cannot love someone, then at least do them no harm.
2. Never do for others what they can and should do for themselves (except as an occasional special surprise).
3. Take time to listen to people. Try to get a feel for what it's like to be in their shoes.
4. Validate the feelings of others by letting them know in a nonjudgmental way that you understand what they're feeling.
5. Take the first step in risking with people. Share something about yourself when appropriate.
6. Empathize with others. Share with them times when you have felt what they're feeling.
7. Learn to affirm people. Let them know that you like them and appreciate them for what they do.
8. Learn to ask for what you need. Let other people know what you would like them to do for you to love you as you would like to be loved.
9. Have fun! Find things to enjoy and laugh about.
10. Always be honest, except when to do so would hurt another.
11. When you need to confront someone, leave personality out of the discussion. Talk about the problem behavior and how it bothers you. Ask for behavior change, and thank the other person if she or he agrees to this. If she or he does not agree to change, decide what you will do to take care of yourself (not to punish the other).
12. When disagreeing with others, make every effort to listen to them to learn the assumptions and values that influence their opinions. Share your own assumptions, values, and opinions. If you cannot find common ground upon which to agree, then agree to disagree.
13. When people insult or criticize you, do not counter in a like manner. Ask them why they feel the way they do. If their feelings are based on a wrong you have done them,

apologize and make amends. If they accuse you unjustly, simply deny your guilt and share your feelings about this. If they persist in their criticism, remain silent and walk away.

14. Forgive other people the wrongs they have done you. Hold nothing against anyone. Resentment hurts you more than it does them.

There can be no love without choice. How would you like it if someone said he loved you because he had to, because he feared the pains of hell? Spare me such a friend, O Lord. "Spare me such a friend, O human."

CARRYING YOUR CROSSES

There is no true spiritual growth without the cross of Christ. By cross, I mean the inner struggles and difficult circumstances you will experience precisely because you are trying to live a Christian life. When you come to these times, you will feel tempted to give up on the spiritual life, to run away, or to take the easy way out. You will know, however, that to do any of the above will not bring you peace of mind.

It is easy to follow Christ when all is going well. It is also easy to love other people when they are healthy or attractive or kind to you. As Jesus said, even tax collectors and sinners can do this. But what about when all is not going well, when others are sick and ugly, or when people mistreat you? Those are times when the ego-survival values of the False Self system emerge with great energy. Yet, you know that this is the Self that must die if you are to experience the life that Christ brings.

The False Self will be put to death in your refusing to indulge the False Self by embracing your cross and clinging to Christ. Thus, the cross is recognized as the means by which your spiritual life is deepened and purified. This is the great secret of Christianity and the reason for the cross as the symbol of our religion.

This does not mean that carrying the cross is easy! It does mean that your struggles are not in vain; it is worth the effort to persist in living a spiritual life. Many of the saints were so convinced of the transforming power of the cross that they welcomed opposition and struggles with joy.

Simply accepting the difficulties inevitable in living a Christian spiritual life is an excellent way to begin to embrace the cross of Christ. Here are a few additional suggestions:

1. Carrying a cross means that you persist in the effort to love. It does not mean that you must repress your feelings about what is going on in your life. Talk to someone about these struggles. A spiritual director can be a supportive listener while encouraging you to persist in your commitments to love. If you do not process your feelings in a healthy way, you can actually be giving this energy over to the False Self system.

2. Carrying a cross does not mean that you must allow another person to abuse you. If it is possible for you to separate from others during times when they are abusive, then do so.

3. During times of struggle, it is helpful to reflect on why this situation is so difficult for you. The cross reveals us to ourselves, and we usually find that the False Self is at the bottom of our experience of conflict. We have what we don't want, and we want what we don't have. If we can learn this about our attitude, then perhaps we can change those parts of our attitude that are in conflict with love.

4. Pray for the good of the person or situation you are struggling with.
5. Pray for the grace to know and do God's will during this time.

The great enemy lies in the good you
are leaving behind. You know this,
and you want to go back. Move on!
The best is yet to come.

RHYTHM FOR DAILY LIVING

How do we bring everything we've covered in this book into a plan for daily living? This is a great challenge, indeed!

It would be a great mistake—perhaps the greatest of all—to think that living a Christian spiritual life means *doing* all sorts of grand things. Far from it. Spirituality is more concerned with our daily manner of being from which our doing will follow. The exercises we have encouraged in this book are largely in the service of being, rather than of doing.

Still, there are a few things we must do each day to keep our manner of being centered in the Spirit.

1. *Daily prayer.* I recommend starting your day with twenty to thirty minutes of prayer before you read the newspaper or have any kind of mental input. Even if you are not a "morning person," you will find that giving to God the openness of your "morning mind" enables God to plant spiritual seeds that will grow and bear fruit all day long.
2. *Living in the NOW.* God is here, NOW, loving you and all creation. If you are lost in thoughts about the past or future, you are missing the moment of God. Morning prayer

helps you focus on God's loving presence NOW. You can remain in this presence all through the day by calling your attention back to the present moment, by doing fully whatever it is you're doing, and by keeping your heart open to give and receive love.

3. *Spiritual reading.* Feed yourself good spiritual reading for at least fifteen minutes each day. Learn more about your faith, spirituality, personal growth. This kind of reading is not a substitute for prayer.

4. *Daily examen.* End each day with this spiritual exercise.

I consider these four recommendations to be minimal for anyone who would make the spiritual life a top priority. Even so, there will surely be some who will say that they have no time for prayer or spiritual reading or examen, or that these are disciplines more appropriate for professional religious than for laypeople. Such people do not neglect to feed their bodies, however, or to waste hours each day watching television and indulging other worldly, superficial pursuits. If you wish to grow in the Spirit, you must likewise feed your spirit. This is as true for laypeople as for religious.

A few words about television are in order here. Surely, this invention has done far more to change patterns in American family life than anything else in the last thirty years. It has been my observation that the more one grows spiritually, the less one is inclined to watch television—or, if one does watch it, he or she discovers that television (and radio, too, for that matter) is a major source of mental agitation and emotional stimulation, both of which are obstacles to nourishing prayer.

The human brain did not develop in a context of hours and hours of watching television. Consequently, the mind requires hours to unravel the meaning of all the input from a couple of programs and all the commercials. In addition, it seems that television programming plays to the least common denominators in intelligence and values. Educational programming and a few weekly series are exceptions but, in general, mental and spiritual life will be greatly weakened in one who watches hours of television each day.

As you consider developing a daily rhythm for growing in the Spirit, examine the role of television and radio in your life. If you spend hours watching television each day, would you be willing to reduce this time in exchange for deepening your spiritual growth or volunteering your services in some manner? The results will amaze you!

Considering all of the foregoing, draw up your own plan for daily living. Talk about it with your spiritual directors and evaluate it from time to time to discern what is the best way for you to live. What works at one time in life might not work during another. The spiritual life is always growing and changing, and you must adapt yourself accordingly.

> Y*ou can do something only, always, in the* NOW. *What you cannot do* NOW, *leave alone. Drop it! Simply drop it! Come back to* NOW. *It's all there is.*

TRACKING THE SPIRITUAL JOURNEY

One way to chart the spiritual journey is to follow its development through various stages of prayer. These stages are described below. They seem to apply to most people, although there are many exceptions to this general pattern.

Active prayer: Sometimes called *discursive prayer,* active prayer includes all forms of prayer that we initiate through the use of our mental faculties (such as thinking, reasoning, imagining, acts of will, visualization, remembering). The following is a typical description of progression in active prayer:

- *Sacred reading*
- *Meditation on the reading* (intellectual and imaginative reflection; recognizing and applying principles; resolutions)
- *Affective prayer* (petitions, thanksgiving, intercession, remorse, praise, adoration)
- *Simplicity, simple regard, centering prayer* (usually follows affective prayer and consists of simple acts of the will to focus lovingly on God and to give God consent to live and act in the Soul)

Infused prayer: This is contemplative prayer, properly speaking. Here the Soul is embraced by God without exercising the faculties. God communicates Spirit-to-spirit, as it were. Generally, contemplative prayer begins as a natural development from the life of active prayer, which helps to prepare the faculties of the Soul to receive the gift of contemplation. It should be known that the stages of contemplative union described below refer not only to experiences during times of prayer but also to times when one is not in formal prayer. They are states of being rather than prayer experiences, per se.

- *Prayer of quiet* (God is united with the deeper levels of the will, but the faculties of thinking, imagination, and sensation remain untouched by this contemplation and often roam about freely. Nevertheless, one is aware of being embraced by God.)
- *Prayer of union* (The union between the Soul and God includes the mental and sensual faculties, which rest quietly during this prayer. In this beautiful state, one experiences the certitude of God's presence and

is delivered from weariness and tedium. God refreshes the Soul so completely that one scarcely experiences the need for sleep and would prefer to spend time resting in union with God. There is no loss of conscious awareness in this prayer.)

- *Prayer of ecstatic union* (Many, but not all, Christian mystics evidence this state. In ecstasy, the Soul is so completely united with God that all self-awareness is lost, along with sensory awareness and consciousness of space and time. The activities of the corporal Soul are diminished so that the Soul, in a partly body-free state, may more fully contemplate the love and beauty of God. The consequences of this prayer are many, including deep inner healing and great virtue. It should be known, however, that there are other experiences of ecstasy besides contemplative ones. Psychic and occult ecstasies may also be found. The mere fact of ecstasy is no indication of mystical contemplation or holiness.)

- *Transforming union* (There is no longer any obstacle in the Soul to receiving the graces of God, so life proceeds in full union between the Soul and God. All the faculties are trained to cooperate with the Holy Spirit and, in turn, they are infused with the loving energies of the Spirit to function according to the will of God. Now something of an "ordinary state" returns, although one is never without the immediate experience of God's loving presence. The Soul continues to learn and grow but in full union with God. This is the fully liberated Soul, that already enjoys something of the wonder of heaven while on this earth. Sin is still a possibility but is generally avoided.)

Transition from active prayer to infused contemplation: As already noted, one begins the spiritual journey by practicing active forms of prayer, and contemplative prayer eventually emerges spontaneously. In describing this transition from active to contemplative prayer, Saint John of the Cross gives three signs to validate this experience. These signs are paraphrased below:

1. One no longer seems to gain any sense of closeness to God through the practice of active prayer.
2. One is not sick nor lukewarm in faith nor in sin but is still drawn to spirituality and desirous of spiritual growth.
3. One enjoys being in God's presence in general loving awareness, without any particular discursive knowledge or awareness.

The first two signs indicate that one is no longer growing through the practice of active prayer forms but that this is not due to spiritual neglect or lack of discipline. The third sign, however, indicates the actual beginnings of contemplation, probably as the prayer of quiet. Saint John encourages one in this situation to diminish the amount of time spent in active prayer and to enjoy the general, loving awareness of God.

It may happen that some experience the first two signs but not the third. What should you in this situation do? The answer is to continue to live a life of faith and love, praying as best you can. A regular practice of centering prayer can help prepare you to receive the gift of contemplation, but a much better preparation comes from your efforts to love other people. Contemplation is a union of love between God and the Soul that overflows to the intellectual and sensual faculties. Therefore, love (not knowledge or ascetical practices) is the best preparation for contemplation, and the best way to live, at any rate. A saint is not judged according to the degree of contemplative prayer evidenced but according to the love he or she has shown.

Dark Nights of the Soul: During the process of spiritual growth, one goes through many changes as a direct result of the deepening union between God and the Soul. Saint John of the Cross spoke of these transformational experiences as *Dark Nights of the Soul.* They are called "Dark Nights" because the light of God pouring into the Soul is of such brilliance and purity that the Soul cannot fully perceive it, so it seems to be a "dark light." Also, this light illuminates all the hidden and dark energies of the Soul, bringing to awareness one's sinfulness and poverty of spirit.

Two Dark Nights are usually recognized, although some authors describe more. These Nights are general descriptions of the spiritual transformation process. Some people can identify with these Nights; others who are obviously progressing seem to experience very few of these characteristics. Each person is unique, and so is each journey. Nevertheless, a knowledge of the Dark Nights may help some to better name, validate, and accept their experiences. It is with these ends in mind that I include the following brief descriptions of the two "Dark Nights" of Saint John of the Cross.

1. *Night of the Senses.* Almost all who make a serious commitment to prayer will come upon this Night within a few months to a couple of years, according to Saint John. This Night generally signals the transition from active to contemplative prayer and is characterized by the three signs listed above. With the beginnings of contemplative prayer, one may experience deep emotional pains that had been repressed. Depression and neurotic tendencies may also surface as the Spirit works with the emotional level of the Soul to cleanse it of pain and enable it to give and receive

love more freely. There is a certain serenity and even joy along with these pains, which encourages one to persist in this Night and which distinguishes these pains from psychopathologies not related to spiritual growth. Generally, this Night lasts several months to two years. Its fruit is emotional healing, love of God, deepening contemplation, and a new ego structure better adapted to life in the Spirit. Because of the pains of this Night, however, many turn away from the spiritual journey at this point and enter into a period of complacency regarding their spiritual needs.

2. *Night of the Spirit.* The courageous Soul that has been through the Night of the Senses may eventually be led into this night. Here the deepest roots of one's unhealthy attitudes are uprooted and cleansed. Indeed, the entire rational and volitional life is thoroughly cleansed of all that is incompatible with life in the Spirit. This Night brings total liberation from the tyranny of the False Self and establishes one in Transforming Union. Such excellent fruit, however, cannot be tasted without going through the mental anguish and energy upheavals that characterize this Night. In many ways, however, it is not as emotionally painful as the Night of the Senses, for the former Night brought peace and stability to the emotional levels. According to Saint John, this Night is purgatory on earth. The Soul that does not undergo this Night on earth will have to do so in the afterlife—unless it is bound for hell, of course. After going through this Night, which may last for years, the Soul experiences something of the joys of heaven while on this earth. The energies of the Soul are thoroughly infused with the loving energies of the Spirit so that the Soul manifests the gifts of the Holy Spirit in abundance.

Note: For a comprehensive discussion of the Nights, see *Invitation to Love: The Way of Christian Contemplation* by Thomas Keating (Element Books, 1992). Father Keating calls these Nights the Divine Therapy, for they heal the Soul more completely than any human psychotherapy could possibly hope to accomplish.

The drop that falls into the ocean
becomes one with the ocean. It becomes
diffused—still itself, now, too, the ocean.
It is simply no longer itself-as-drop,
but is now itself-in-ocean.

7

HOW TO *BE*
A MYSTIC

———

Intellectuals who write about mysticism are like men who write about pregnancy: They can say a lot of things that are true, but they do not know the Relationship, the Unity, the Experience. Better to be pregnant with God than to be a theological obstetrician.

okay, I'll grant you that the title of this chapter is probably a bit misleading. Being a mystic is not a skill you can learn like, say, playing golf or crocheting. It's not a *doing* thing at all, but a *being*. And so the word "be" is emphasized in the title, rather than "How to." See what I mean?

Learning to "be" might be a new idea for you, especially if you've been conditioned (like almost everyone else) to believe that your worth as a human being is determined primarily by what you do. To be: How would you do this? Oops! There's that word again: "do." How natural for us to ask, What must we *do* to *be*."

Well, the answer, of course is: *nothing*. We can "do" nothing to learn to *be* for the simple reason that we already *are*, before we *do* anything. Doing doesn't create being, but comes out of it. For us to do anything, there must first be someone to do it, which tells us that being is greater than doing. Our doing will never totally exhaust our being.

What is called for then is a shift of consciousness—what Scripture calls a *metanoia*—so that our sense of self does not come from our doing, but is immediately and mysteriously present to us anytime we want to tune into it. This is a whole new way of seeing, or being awake, and it ultimately affects all our doing kinds of things.

In this chapter, I set forth a variety of meditations and exercises to help facilitate this shift of consciousness. These exercises are in no particular order, and some are philosophical, some practical, some intuitive. Use what is helpful, and ignore the rest. Good luck!

ANTHROPOLOGY

What does it really mean to be aware? Here is an attempt to describe the human act of awareness.

1. Awareness is. It cannot be reduced to simpler components.
2. What *is* awareness? Who knows! Perhaps it is the light of the Soul; God; the True Self. Who knows! What awareness is cannot be defined. *That* awareness is cannot be denied.
3. For most people, awareness is colored by desires, which are, in turn, generated by emotional states such as insecurity, shame, resentment. Desires arise to compensate for

these pains. Ignorant thinking based on irrational beliefs about the Self and reality keep one caught up in desire. Thus, for most, awareness is introverted and caught up in preoccupation over the fulfillment of desires.

4. When awareness is colored by pain, then the world and others are seen through a filter of desires: as being for or against the attainment of our desires. This is the origin of friends and enemies, of good and bad, of love and hate.

5. When awareness is colored by emotional pain and desires, the attender in consciousness is a small Self, a self-concerned "I." This "I" experiences itself as real, owing to the felt reality of the emotions and desires that keep it preoccupied, the behaviors that proceed from its decisions, and the ripples these behaviors cause in the world.

6. When awareness is freed from desire, there is no small "I." Rather, the attender is synonymous with awareness itself and with all sensations, thoughts, and feelings that enter the field of awareness. Such awareness is limited only by the body's fixation in time and space.

7. In the state of pure, or cosmic, attention, sensory perception is uncontaminated by thoughts, feelings, and desires. There is just seeing, hearing, smelling, and touching. Feelings come and go, but they do not disrupt sensory perception.

8. Will can be used to focus awareness, to concentrate and intensify awareness in a certain direction. Volitional awareness is defined as paying attention.

9. When the will is open to relationship and engagement in life, attention is also opened to become cosmic and pure. This openness of the will is called *agape*. Agape is the only stance that maintains the will in openness and awareness in purity.

10. Lack of openness to relationship results in contraction of the will and, hence, a constriction of attention. Therefore,

openness to loving relationship with all is the only anti-
dote to the misery of the small Self.

11. Rational thinking directs the will. The will focuses awareness. Awareness presents data to the rational mind. These
are the three irreducible and interrelated dynamics of consciousness. They are the spiritual qualities of human beings, incarnated in a body, conditioned and formed in a
body in a culture, and freed from the limitations of the
body at death.

12. The assault of evil is directed against reason. If people can
be convinced that they need lots of irrelevant things or
that they can be okay only if others approve them, or that
they must be perfect and in control to be safe, then they
will live in insecurity. This contracts the will and constricts
attention. This is the meaning of sin.

13. There is no liberation for the ignorant, for those who can
be persuaded to be fearful, for those who do not value
their worth, for those who hold on to resentments. Their
rational intelligence is distorted. Their attention is narrow
and defensive. Where there is ignorance, there is superfici-
ality and lack of wholeness: a fallen creature.

14. The struggle to know truth is a struggle to free the will
and awareness from the ensnarements of evil.

15. Freedom from ignorance does not lie in accumulating information, but in knowing truth.

16. Truth is that toward which reason tends when one lives
with one's own questions, honors these questions, and
struggles to answer them honestly.

17. In the struggle to answer one's questions, the mind is tamed,
the will is directed toward its proper end, and awareness
is progressively expanded.

18. The final Truth is nonconceptual mystery—just as the origin of awareness and will cannot be defined. The final
Truth is ineffable; it cannot be contained. This does not

mean that Truth is an illusion, or that the struggle to know Truth is a waste of time. It means only that Truth is not-knowing as well as knowing. It means that Truth is "seen" in awareness, and loved with the will, even as it is grasped by reason.

19. The three movements in the spiritual life are clear: (1) recognition of one's condition by practicing honesty; (2) resolution of one's emotional pain through forgiveness; and (3) retraining the mind to meet one's true needs by striving to understand truth and practicing loving relationship skills.

20. In summary: Awareness "sees" the activities of the will and intellect, and is, in turn, freed by their loving direction.

T he True Self is the one who is here through all the changes in life. To identify with any of life's changing circumstances and experiences is to lose the True Self to a "my" self. The True Self is not "mine." It is just-me.

ENLIGHTENMENT

How does awareness lead to true enlightenment? Here are some observations.

1. In the lower, egoic states, awareness is identified with and reflected by self-concept. Intelligence and will, too, are bound up in self-concept. This is the small Self, or mental ego.

2. The ego can be seen "from the outside" by a greater See-er, such as in a dream, where one sees and feels oneself. Who is this great See-er? Who is this unborn, serene Attender-of-my-life? It is the True Self. It is the sun seeing its sunbeam.

3. The True Self is the deepest subject of awareness. It is a direct experience of oneself as subject. This subjectivity is identical with awareness, and not inferior to it in any way.

4. The small self, or ego, is the object of awareness, a reflection of oneself, a self-image. The ego is awareness emotionally bonded to self-concept. It is reflexive consciousness.

5. In the True Self state, awareness, reason, and will are one. Awareness is intelligently loving. Intelligence is lovingly aware. Love is intelligently aware. Nonreflectively, nonconceptually so.

6. To live in the True Self state is to be here/now/in-love, without distraction, without reflection, without reservation. This is ecstasy, for it is being-in-God.

7. Everyone experiences the True Self state in moments of ecstasy. The problem is that we believe external circumstances and material substances account for our ecstasies. Thus do we try to replicate the experience through these circumstances and things. We need only drop the "I want," and there is ecstasy.

8. The "I" cannot be dropped as long as ignorance, shallowness, emotional pain, desires, and addictions still persist.

9. As the mind is being healed and retrained, the True Self state emerges gradually, becoming more and more a *permanent state* as our growth and healing progress.

10. In the True Self state, happiness is unconditioned by any external contingencies. To maintain the True Self state, one need only stop disturbing oneself. Happiness exists when the mind stops creating unhappiness.

11. It is rare that one lives in the True Self state constantly

each day. Even the best of saints fall. But these falls are the exception, not the norm. The saint gets up, forgives, and moves on.

12. When others see a True Self, they see only an ordinary person. Looking more attentively, others will note the ease and serenity that characterize the movements of a True Self. Through the True Self's actions, the beauty of God's incarnate Word is revealed.

13. In the True Self, we are simply human. We are also God-manifesting-as-the-person-we-are. This is what it means to be human.

14. In the True Self, the See-er sees all things. In being seen, all things are changed. What is Real is validated, loved, and energized. What is unreal falls away.

15. In the True Self, a person is a chakra, an energy organ through which God sees and loves and knows himself in creation. The organ is real. It may distort or constrict the Light. But the organ is not the Light. It is illuminated.

16. All people—indeed, all creation—are Light-manifestors. If they are not manifesting Light, it is because intelligence and will are distorted. Even the innocent creation can be so distorted by people. How ridiculous, the behavior of a "trained watchdog."

17. The True Self "knows," without knowing how it knows what it knows. It can explain its insights in terms of concepts familiar to the intellect, but it does not know how it has arrived at these insights. They come into the mind like air into the nose. It is as though the mind now participates in a larger MIND, as a brain cell participates in the life of the mind.

In the end, there are only two considerations that matter: Agape, and non-Agape. Are you here/now, open, willing to give of yourself, open to receiving and enjoying others and creation? If not, you are in non-Agape, constricting attention, desiring, cultivating self-states of consciousness-anxiety.

CHRISTOLOGY

Christ is the key, the center. Here are some perspectives on Him as seen in the process of spiritual growth.

1. Christ is a vessel through which Light shines clearly. To look to him is to be drawn to Light.
2. Christ is Teacher and Model who focuses the will and intelligence in the Light.
3. Christ is Risen Guru. He is available to all who seek him.
4. Christ is Eucharist. We consume him, and so become part of him. He absorbs us into his Body by becoming part of our own.
5. Christ is Yogi. He yokes himself to his followers and moves them to undertake disciplines of transformation.
6. Christ is Heart-Master. Contact with him communicates the grace of his heart to the heart of the devotee. He gratuitously gives devotees an experience of his own life, imprinting his life in the mind. By loving him, we become like him.
7. Christ is Son of the Father. He transforms his followers to see as he sees. His followers see with his own eyes, recognizing creation to be gift of the Father.

8. Christ is Redeemer. He accomplishes in us what we could never accomplish on our own, raising us from the pit of ego-bondage, to experience his own, magnificent Light.
9. Christ is the Ground of the Soul of my neighbor. Do I know this? Do I act accordingly?
10. Christ is Victor over evil. He strips it of its terror, revealing its destiny to be empty.
11. Christ is Risen. There is no permanent death. This life is a stage of growth.
12. Christ is Friend, ever-approachable, ever-interested, ever-present, to those who call upon him in faith.
13. Christ is God's blessing to this world, and reassurance that we have not been forgotten.

*If union with God is the ideal, then
it must be admitted that this union must
take place here/now, for that is where
God is, and it must be in-love,
for that is how God is.*

MYSTICAL THEOLOGY

How do we see and understand God at the very deepest level of our being? Here are some thoughts on how this stage of reflection/contemplation is experienced.

1. Just as the body is already in the Soul and the Soul in the body, so, too, God is already in the Soul, and the Soul is in God.
2. God is always present to the Soul, giving it life, loving it, attempting to lead it to become what God has created it to be.

3. Attachments and addictions create disturbances in the Soul that prevent one from knowing God's presence and responding to the leadings of the Holy Spirit.

4. Nevertheless, even in this state of disturbance, one can begin to relate to God in whatever way is most meaningful. Jesus Christ is God's invitation to a return to full union.

5. When we love God and others while dropping attachments and addictions, the False Self will be put to death and the True Self born. This is a painful process—a cross that heals the Soul.

6. Through the Dark Nights of transformation, the Soul is drawn into deeper and deeper realms of silence that transcend thought and feeling. Here, God's presence is known intuitively, and the Soul becomes increasingly free to follow the leadings of the Spirit without being disturbed by attachments, addictions, and other worldly influences.

7. Thus it is that the Soul is divinized, or made able to know God as Christ knows God. This is the fruit of the spiritual journey and the reason for which we were created.

Contemplation is joining templates— Christ's loving openness with my own attention. Rest in him and be healed.

AFFIRMATIONS FOR REALIZING THE TRUE SELF

Affirmations are small prayers or sayings that positively express the authentic self. These statements can help hoax the True Self out of hiding. Repeat each of these affirmations slowly, mindfully, attempting to experientially comprehend the truth in each.

"I am the one who is here/now, alive in this moment."

"I am the one who is reading these words, seeing out of these eyes."

"I am the one who is loved by God in this very moment."

"I am because you have made me, O Lord."

"I am here, now, freely willing to love."

"I am not my thoughts; I am not my feelings; I am not my desires; I am not what others think I am—I am the one who *has* thoughts, feelings, desires. I am the one whom others see."

"I am, and others are, too. I am me; they are themselves."

"I am, and it is very good to be. Thank You, Lord."

The one who looks, the looking, and the seeing are one: How beautiful! "When the eye is single, the whole body will be sound." How true!

8

EXERCISES FOR
BREAKING FREE

When the water in the pond is calm,

the dirt settles, and one can see

the bottom.

When the mind is free from

disordered desires,

the True Self can shine forth.

this chapter offers some methods which I have found helpful in breaking free from the clutches of misapplied desires, sorting through the chaff of the False Self, and finding the genuine. The exercises include an attitude check, an awareness evaluation, affirmations for inner transformation, guided meditations, a plan for Christian prayer, and other strategies as well.

HOW TO DISTURB YOURSELF MOST OF THE TIME: AN AWARENESS EXERCISE

Often we do not see the disordered thinking that clutters and creates obstacles on our path to spiritual growth. By doing a bit of "reverse thinking" we might finally perceive how deeply rooted are our negative thoughts and perceptions.

- Think about all the possible negative things that might happen to you and your loved ones. Dwell on these negatives!
- Tell yourself that you're not okay now—that the circumstances of your life are not right for you to experience serenity and happiness, or that you'll be okay when... (but not now).
- Spend lots of time thinking judgmental thoughts about yourself and other people. Dwell on your own and others' negative qualities.
- Be a perfectionist. Have lots and lots of "shoulds" in your head regarding yourself and others. Then you can do all of the above most of the time.
- Tell yourself you need other people's approval and admiration. Spend lots of time thinking about how to get this.
- Try to control the behavior of other people. This one's guaranteed.
- Watch competitive sports on television. Strongly identify with one specific team, and get emotionally involved in the games.
- Watch lots of television and listen to the radio. Keep your environment filled with such noise. Avoid silence at all costs.

- Nurture a grudge against someone. Fantasize all kinds of ways to put that person in his or her place.
- Stay in an unhealthy relationship. Be a victim! "It's God's will."
- Eat junk food, drink alcohol, lots of coffee an/or high-sugar beverages.
- Keep expanding your material wants. How dare the "Joneses" show you and your family up.
- Cut down on your sleep. Stay up late at night watching television or reading trashy novels.
- Don't exercise! Be a couch potato.
- Avoid contact with the outdoors and nature. Who needs fresh air!
- Be very attached to your own good opinion of yourself. Take your idea of yourself very seriously, and get defensive if other people don't properly adore you.
- Believe that life has no meaning...that death has the last word.
- Avoid prayer at all costs. Or, if you do pray, spend most of your time telling God what you want instead of listening to what God wants. Then, get angry at God when you don't get what you asked for, and use this anger to justify yourself against God.

If you want anything more than to be-here-now-in-love-to-love, you will not be happy, but in a state of disordered desiring.

ATTITUDE CHECK

Here is a set of questions that will aid you in an attitude examination. You may want to respond to these questions on a separate sheet of paper or in a personal journal.

1. What do you want from God?
2. What feelings are you in touch with?
3. What preoccupying thoughts have you been holding? What feelings are attached to them?
4. How's your breathing? Are you able to relax and center in the navel plexus?
5. Have you been shaking your legs? What are they telling you?
6. Are you seeking a "fix" in your prayer and meditation?
7. What has been the quality of your awareness?
8. Have you been focusing on loving or on being loved?

*R**ight practice—loving* NOW*—is far more important than anything else. This practice is happiness itself. It leads to understanding, not vice versa.*

AFFIRMATIONS FOR A LOVING ATTITUDE

Use these affirmations to improve your attitude and focus more clearly in a positive manner. It is best to speak these affirmations with the lips (even quietly, as in a whisper) rather than simply to repeat them mentally. They may also be used with the imagination, to envision yourself speaking these words to another person or to hear God speaking these words to you.

As you meditate with these affirmations, you may discover feelings that tend to support the affirmation being expressed. Allow this to happen, for it will help you carry forward your resolve. You may also discover attitudes and feelings that seem to go against the direction of the affirmation. Observe this and feel it, but don't get involved in willfully trying to reverse these sentiments. Simply persevere in your meditation with these affirmations, and in time old emotional attitudes will be reversed.

God affirming you: In prayer, imagine God standing before you, speaking.

- "I am here for you, no matter where you may be."
- "I am here with you, no matter what you may feel."
- "You are always acceptable to me, no matter what other people (or you) may think about you."
- "I see and appreciate the many good things you do each day."
- "I see and appreciate your good intentions, even when you fail to carry them out with your behavior."
- "I see your ill-intentions and behavior, but I love you all the same and forgive you everything even before you ask."
- "I see your stubbornness and unwillingness to change, but I will wait forever if that's how long it takes for you to respond to my love."
- "I am here to serve you unto happiness."

Affirmations expressing love for another person: Envision this person in some manner, and speak these words to the person with your mind.

- "I wish you peace, joy, and well-being."
- "You are always acceptable to me, regardless of your behavior."
- "I am here to serve you unto happiness, in whatever way is appropriate."
- "I see and appreciate the many good things you do each day."
- "I do not know your heart or intentions, so I do not

judge you, even when your behavior is out of line."

- "I forgive you every wrong you have done me, and I ask that you forgive me as well."
- "Even if you do not return my love, I will still love you and hope in you."

Affirmations for healthy boundaries in relationships: Envision a person and speak these words to this person in your mind.

- "I decide what I am willing to do or not do for you and another."
- "I have a right to say no to you when my needs take precedence."
- "I have a right to ask for anything I want in a relationship, but I leave you free to respond."
- "I allow you to make your own decisions." (Note: Parents must be involved in helping their children make decisions.)
- "I allow you to make mistakes and suffer the consequences."
- "I am willing to confront behavior that bothers me and to take measures to protect myself from unnecessary hurt."

Affirmations and self-image: Read these affirmations slowly and prayerfully in solitude and silence. You may also write them in your journal just before sleep for a deeper impact. Spend at least twenty minutes with them each day until your negative self-talk becomes minimal.

- "If God is for me, who can be against me?"
- "I am lovable and acceptable because I exist—because God is choosing to love me into existence in this now-moment, and God doesn't make junk."

- "I know how to do many things that can contribute to the improvement of the human community. If I do not share my giftedness, it will be missed by others."
- "I do not judge myself as a bad person when I make mistakes or deviate from a social norm."
- "I do not judge myself as a bad person when I hurt another with my behavior. I take responsibility for my behavior and make amends."
- "It is unreasonable for me to expect perfection of myself. I will do the best I can, and that is all that God expects."
- "I accept my physical appearance. If others reject me on this basis, it is not because I am unlovable but because they are comparing my appearance to a social norm propagated largely by the media."
- "I accept all of my feelings, pleasant and unpleasant, knowing that I am more than my feelings. Feelings come and go. They do not reveal to me my true worth as a person. I do not define myself on the basis of my feelings but on my faith convictions."
- "Other people have judged me and mistreated me, and this has affected my view of myself. I am more than what others have told me I am, so I do not accept their judgments of me."
- "I forgive everyone for everything they have done that has hurt me, for I know that holding on to hurt and resentment will keep me from growing to be the person God created me to be."
- "I take responsibility for meeting my own needs in a moral and loving manner. It is not someone else's responsibility to meet my needs."
- "I am in doubt about my beauty and worth. I ask God to help me to see and know myself as God sees and knows me."

- "Right now, I am where I should be in life. I have learned many lessons and have many more to learn. That is life: learning and growing. It is good for me to be here in life."

- "Right now I have everything I need to be as happy as it is possible for me to be in this life. Therefore, I renounce the idea that my present circumstances are inadequate for happiness, that I need more of something or another, or that I need less of something or another. Happiness is an attitude, not an acquisition. In gratitude to God, I accept myself and my life just as they are."

*D*o not "put on" or imitate anyone—
not even the Lord Jesus Christ (apologies
to Saint Paul). Instead, be-here/now/in-love,
with your whole being awake, relaxed,
intellect alert, memory available if needed,
the heart ready to love. Do this as you,
not someone else.

AN EXERCISE FOR INNER HEALING

Use the following statements and questions to work toward an inner transformation that will help heal emotional hurts. Each statement or question is a step in the process, so don't skip any. You may wish to write your reaction/answer to each step in your journal.

1. Pay attention to the kinds of thoughts, feelings, and images going on in your consciousness.
2. Identify preoccupations that seem to convey the theme "I'll

be okay when..." Label all of these as specifically as possible, that is, "I'll be okay when I lose twenty pounds."

3. Restate the preoccupation in a negative sense, e. g., "I'm
not okay because I'm twenty pounds overweight."

4. How do you feel about this "not being okay because...,"
for example, "...because I'm overweight, I feel embarrassed
and ashamed"?

5. What are specific circumstances when you have felt this
way, for example, "I feel ashamed and embarrassed about
my weight when I go to family gatherings or parties"?
Allow yourself to feel these feelings.

6. What do you need from God, from yourself, or from other
people when you feel this way, for example, "When I feel
ashamed and 'fat,' I need to know that I am still loved and
valued as a person"?

7. Invite the Holy Spirit to speak to you and console you in
your feelings of pain. Pray for the grace to be healed from
these painful emotions. (See Rom 8:35–39; Jn 14:27–31;
Mt 11:28–30.)

8. Allow yourself to feel loved even in your pain.

9. Self-affirm yourself. From your conscious, rational self,
speak a nurturing phrase to your emotional experience,
for example, "I'm a lovable person." "You [inner child]
are loved by me, no matter what."

10. Engage in positive imaging. See yourself in a circumstance
usually difficult for you, and feel yourself as a loving, lovable person in this circumstance. Repeat your affirmation
if necessary.

Careful what you say and think.
Careful about the thoughts you hold
on to, for they shape your experience
of attention and energy.

THE NATURE OF ATTACHMENTS

This section reviews the nature of attachments, desires, and additions, and gives benchmarks for the identification of the presence.

Desire: attraction of the will toward any particular person, place, or thing. It is natural and inevitable for a created being with needs to have desires. Our deepest, most fundamental desires are to live, to understand, and to be happy; these desires, however, can ultimately be fulfilled only in God.

Disordered desires: inappropriate attraction of the will toward any particular person, place, or thing. A disordered desire is to have what you do not want (but what you cannot be rid of without violating your moral values) or to want what you do not have (in such a manner as to undermine your experience of what you need most, that is, union with God). The fulfillment of such a desire hurts oneself or others; the pursuit of such a desire violates moral values. The cultivation of such a desire undermines the experience of God as the fulfillment of our deepest desire.

Attachments: disordered desires that have become more or less habitual preoccupations of the mind and will. Examples of attachments include trying to gain the approval of others, winning, controlling other people and circumstances, accumulating money or sexual experience, getting high on something, doing perfect work, losing weight. Attachments leave our intellect preoccupied with ways to get what we want and avoid what we don't want; other people are seen as a help or a hindrance to obtaining attachment; we become judgmental and our will is focused on getting what we want: selfishness. Our emotional climate is disturbed; we feel anxiety about not get-

ting what we want, and angry toward threats to our fulfillment. Our attention is focused on the past and the future, and
the NOW is missed. The experience of God is as One who can
help us get what we want.

Addictions: attachments that have become compulsive preoccupations. The mind and will are no longer capable of completely resisting indulgence.

The spiritual significance of attachments and addictions: They
are our primary obstacle to experiencing peace, happiness, and
union with God.

We have attachments or addictions

- if we experience anxiety over situations beyond our
  control
- if our mind is "noisy," preoccupied over concerns
  from which we derive little pleasure
- if we find it difficult to enjoy the NOW because disturbing memories from the past or anxious concerns
  about the future intrude

To drop our attachments or addictions we can

- notice anxious preoccupations and their major
  themes, and verbalize these to God
- say the Serenity Prayer and ask God to care for specific things not within our control, to give us the grace
  to trust in God's providence in our life
- bring our attention into the NOW and do what we're
  doing. The anxious preoccupation will fall away in
  short order if we do not indulge it behaviorally or
  mentally

For especially stubborn attachments and addictions we can

- notice our preoccupation and its major themes: "I feel anxious about...because..."
- turn each theme into a question: "How can I be sure that...?" "What should I say to impress So-and-so?" "How can I be sure I will have enough money?"
- see how much this question has influenced our thinking and behavior by making a list of past decisions and behavior related to this question; asking God for the grace to be free of this disordered desire
- list the ways in which this behavior has affected ourselves and others
- resolve to make amends where our behavior in reference to this issue has hurt another, and ask God for forgiveness (perhaps in the form of the sacrament of reconciliation)
- ask ourselves: "What real need (if any) is this question addressing?"
- find appropriate or prudent ways to meet this need
- see ourselves meeting this need in an appropriate manner. (Ask for divine guidance to see how to do this, and to desire this kind of responsible behavior.)
- see and acknowledge preoccupations, especially old ones, nonjudgmentally, but not indulging them. (This is the true meaning of abstinence: bringing our attention into the NOW and doing what we're doing. If it is time to meet our real need in the manner we decided on in the previous point, we can go ahead and do so in awareness and gratitude.)

When all else fails: After we've been doing the above for some time, it may become obvious that a compulsive attachment is so deeply rooted that we need additional help. We should not hesitate to ask for it. Help is available in the various Twelve Step groups and in addiction-treatment programs.

THE SERENITY PRAYER: A MEDITATION

This exercise is a meditative and healing summary of the Serenity Prayer.

God, grant me the serenity to accept the things I cannot change,

- What are the chief causes of my anxieties?
- Do I have any control over these people, things, circumstances?
- Am I willing to let go of what I cannot control?

the courage to change the things I can,

- What do I control?
- What can I do about my situation?
- Because I can always control my attitude—the way I relate to people, places, things, circumstances—how do I need to change my attitude?

and the wisdom to know the difference.

- Knowing what is my business, the other person's business, and God's business is hard.
- If I cannot control or change something, I need to let it go.
- I ask God to help me do so in trust.

Living one day at a time, enjoying one moment at a time.

- Am I now/here?
- If I am not now/here, am I no/where?
- I ask the grace to be attentive to the NOW in loving readiness.

Accepting hardships as the pathway to peace. Taking, as he did, this sinful world as it is, not as I would have it.

- My cross is the burden that loving commitment has brought me.
- Do I accept my crosses?
- Do I see how rejecting them makes me and others miserable?
- Do I know that crosses lead to growth?

Trusting that he will make all things right
if I surrender to his will,

- Do I trust him to care for things if I let go of control?
- Have I yet learned that his plans for me are best?
- Do I believe that in his will is my happiness?
- I ask for a growth in faith.

that I may be reasonably happy in this life,

- Happiness is a consequence of living-here-now-in-love. Am I unconditionally happy?
- Whom do I blame for my unhappiness?
- Do I see that it is the way I react to life that causes happiness and unhappiness?
- I ask the grace to take responsibility for my own happiness.

and supremely happy with him forever.

- "The sufferings of this present time are not worth comparing with the glory about to be revealed to us" (Rom 8:18).
- Do I cling to this life?
- Do I fear death?
- Does the prospect of heaven give me hope and joy?
- I ask for the grace to be hopeful.

DYNAMICS OF THE HEART

Where your treasure is, there is your heart, or center. Where your center is, there are your thoughts and feelings. The "computer mind" connects with the center via an "ultimate question" and is constantly working on this question. As your thoughts and feelings go, so goes your behavior. Behavior is a product of thought, feeling, and centeredness, and reinforces patterns of thought and feeling in a center.

To change your heart, ask yourself the following questions:

- What is my treasure? What does my behavior tell me? What do I feel excited about or drawn toward? What is the question to which my deepest thoughts are responding? What are the values implied in this deepest question? Where does this question come from, e .g., world, parents, the Holy Spirit?
- What have been the consequences to my life and others' in the living out of this question?
- Do I wish to continue living out this question?
- How does this question relate to Christ's questions of me: "Will you let me love you? Will you love me with your whole heart, soul, mind, and strength? Will

you seek first my kingdom? Will you help me build
my kingdom on earth as in heaven?"
- Am I willing to continue placing these questions first,
and resisting the questions/temptations of the world?

Living in the center means

- seeing and resisting all that takes you away from
Christ, calling that by name, identifying the question
it asks, and refusing the behavior
- resolving emotional consequences of uncentered living through forgiveness and making amends
- nourishing mind and heart with good reading, teaching, music, etc.
- growing in the center through prayer, meditation, and
the sacraments

General principles for following your heart include:

- "But strive first for the kingdom of God and his righteousness, and all these things will be given to you"
(Mt 6:33).
- The Principle of synchronicity. You are drawn through
your center to people, circumstances, books, etc., that
deepen your life in that center. This can work for good
or evil.
- When in doubt, place your growth first, and you will
usually end up serving the kingdom as a consequence.
- Never make an important decision when divided
within yourself.
- There is evil; there are forces of darkness that would
like to steer you off your path. Stay awake!
- If something is not true, then it is not about Love.
- Live one day at a time, here/now/in-love. The ques-

tion for each day is: "What would you have me do and learn today, Lord?"

- Examen: "What have I done and learned with you today, Lord?" "How did I stray from our union, Lord?" Note thoughts and feelings that arise in response to these questions. What false questions or issues did you get caught up in? Give praise and thanksgiving for times of union: ask pardon for separations.

*L et the "chooser" step forward,
out of the chatter and rumination, and
let the choice be for here/now/loving-
willingness—God! Then all shall be well.*

GUIDELINES FOR CHRISTIAN PRAYER

Prayer is the significant act of spiritual growth. The following exercise gives a step-by-step method for practicing a form of Christian prayer.

Amplified method of Centering Prayer

1. Allow at least twenty minutes (perhaps after a period of reading and reflecting on Scripture).
2. Find a quiet place where you will not be disturbed by external circumstances.
3. Assume proper posture: back straight, chin parallel to the floor, right hand resting on the left hand. If you can sit on the floor, that is best; if not, a straight-backed chair or a prayer stool will do.
4. Offer your prayer time to God. Ask the Holy Spirit and your guardian angel to lead you in this prayer.

5. Close your eyes, or gaze gently at a place on the floor about three feet in front of you.

6. Become aware of the sensations in your body. Gently scan your body from toes to crown. As you notice your body, imagine that the Light of God is coming into your body through your awareness.

7. Become aware of your breathing. Breathe normally at first, then increase the depth of your breathing, not forcing anything. Inhale into your heart, then draw the breath into the navel area; exhale deeply from the navel area. Imagine that your inhalation is charged with the love of God, and your exhalation is discharging stress and negativity.

8. Simply rest in God's presence, using a simple word or phrase to maintain your openness to God. If you feel moved to complete loving silence, let go of the word or words. (Instead of using a word, you might also imagine that you are bathing in God's Light, and you might "feel" your spirit receiving this Light. You might also simply open to God as a Presence in whom you live and move and have your being.)

9. When you become aware of thoughts that lead you away from this simple resting, return to the previous point. (If you have the gift of glossolalia and it suggests itself during this time of prayer, do give consent to it.)

10. Gently end the prayer experience when you are ready by opening your eyes. It is also good to stand up and walk slowly, right hand resting in the left, noting the feel of your body moving—especially the sensations under your feet. Five minutes of this "walking meditation" is usually sufficient to make the transition from prayer into everyday living. Many find it necessary to wait another fifteen minutes or so before reading or engaging in focused mental concentration. Do not judge the experience according to how you feel right after prayer. The effects are sometimes more obvious hours later.

CHARACTERISTICS OF DETACHMENT

The following goals represent the attitude of the detached and serene person who rests in God's will.

1. To allow no one, no thing, and no circumstance to determine whether you will be happy or not. (NOTE: To be emotionally affected is normal, but do not be emotionally determined by these factors.)
2. To prefer God's will over anything else, believing that your real happiness is to be found in God's will
3. To choose to do God's will as you understand it, regardless of what other people think about you for doing so
4. To fully accept yourself and all your natural desires
5. To pursue your natural desires without attachment and in consideration of moral values

> *Life is not a torment to be endured,*
> *but a journey to be lived one day at a time.*
> *Let each day be new. No projecting onto*
> *tomorrow.*

9

NUGGETS FROM THE STREAM OF LIFE

Proverbs and Practical Wisdom for Spiritual Living

The best theories are only maps. Real meaning does not come from having the best map.

a nugget is a piece of gold "in the raw." It must be melted down and purif ed to yield its treasure. The same may be said of spiritual nuggets like the ones that follow. They are presented "in the raw," each of them needing the fires of your own life to draw out their truths.

Don't rush through these proverbs. Let each speak to your experience to validate and challenge your living. Then will the gold be found deep in your own heart.

"Lost in my thoughts!" So true: That is where most people are.

Anything that intensifies separateness and narrow identification is to be avoided. For example, winning, competitive sports, having, getting, most philosophy and theology, most television programs. Only total passivity to the Life Force within will do. That which obstructs its flow is to be avoided.

◎

When thinking accomplishes nothing, drop it by switching the attention to breathing. Breathe naturally, normally, each breath received in gratitude for the gift of life and for the "Breather" in the Soul.

◎

The intellect is servant, not master. It provides vision, which is necessary. But it cannot be the center in which attention rests, for then it becomes puffed with pride and turns the Self and the world into a conceptual system, which it defends and presides over. This is vanity and great illusion!

◎

You have no shame, but you still have pride! Surprised? Remember this: Pride came before shame in Eden.

◎

The namer has become the named, the hunter caught in his own snare: the False Self.

◎

Paradigmatic "stages of growth" are useful for validating broad, general patterns of human folding. They are maps of sorts, but not as precise as geographical maps. Learn the maps, then put them down and enjoy the scenery. Who would want to look at a map of the Alps when riding through them?

Do not repress memory, but do not cling to it, either. You are at least everything you have experienced. Your past is the record of your song and dance.

◎

If at first you don't succeed, drop the whole idea of success. What's done is done. Move on. A new moment, God NOW.

◎

No roles can maintain the True Self, although it can take on any role and play it in full awareness. The True Self "has" the role, not vice versa.

◎

Creation is that through which God flows. God is the One who flows through creation. Creation needs God. God needs nothing, although without creation, God would have nothing to flow through.

◎

Don't worry about anything—ever! What's done is done and what will be will have to wait until NOW. Make amends if your past haunts you, and make plans if you must. But do it NOW.

◎

Preoccupied? Lots of involuntary thoughts racing around? The data banks are searching. Searching for what? See if there is an issue to which you need to respond. If there is, then make a plan to do something about it and do it when appropriate. If there is no real issue, drop the useless thinking by shifting attention to the now, the senses, creation. Let the thought waves die out gently.

The purpose of thought/speech is to communicate about needs and perceptions. Multiply needs into wants and distort perception and thought increases: the noisy, disturbed mind.

People are not really all that screwed-up! Let them rid themselves of a bit of pain through reconciliation, and loosen the hold on self-image and…there they are: just people.

In the end, attention/energy assumes the form, or thought, of you spoken by God. To let yourself go into the form that God has created you to be is contemplation.

Can there be attention without intention? Can there be intention without attachment? No to the first, yes to the second.

Attention is a light that energizes. What you attend to, you energize. Beware! If you attend too long to temptation, it shall come to pass. If you keep your mind fixed on being-here/now/in-love-to-love, you will always be happy.

Never abandon your common sense or your sense of humor. They will, without fail, keep you from going crazy.

Preoccupation is useless thinking. Useless thinking is thinking about that which does not concern you, that which you cannot change, and that which is not yours to do now. Withdraw your attention from all such useless thinking and you will immediately feel better.

Mind-intent is more important than states of mind. Let states of mind come and go but hold fast to your willingness to love all things.

⊚

Most heresy is very close to the truth—maybe only half a degree off. But this small distortion on a thousand-mile journey leads one far off course. Therefore, do not spurn dogma. It helps you keep your bearings.

⊚

When you talk, read, or write too much, the intellect and speech center can be overstimulated, and mental silence will be lost. This is understandable. How do you think your right arm would feel if you swung it round and round all day?

⊚

Words determine emotional reality. "I don't like living with kids!" produces a much different emotional reaction from "I'm tired right now, and feel bothered by my kids' noises." The second phrase is more honest and produces a less hostile reaction.

⊚

You can experience the other as other only if you want nothing from the other but to give what is needed. When there is desire, the other is seen as for or against its fulfillment—not as a person.

⊚

Thought/speech is a way of communicating and focusing attention and energy through the medium of sound (rather than image).

Paradigmatic conceptualization constricts attention and distorts energy along the lines suggested by the paradigm. This may represent an improvement over emotional consciousness but it is an obstacle to spiritual enlightenment.

Thinking is not the enemy of silence. Useless thinking that conduces toward anxiety, jealousy, shame, or resentment—this is the enemy of silence. It is the thinking of the False Self. Drop it, and the thinking that remains will be enjoyable and useful.

The key to now-living is: "Do what you are doing." This means letting go of what you are not doing or cannot be doing. It is in reflecting, comparing, and judging that the False Self is born, and these operations are starved out when you simply "do what you are doing" and only that. Then, too, psychic energy is transformed, spiritualized, and attention becomes clear and peaceful.

Realize the divine within? You cannot even realize the consciousness of your spouse, whom you see and touch and know so well. Experience the consciousness of another—yes! But this is not the same as realizing another's consciousness.

We receive him and become one with him who is one with the Father in the Spirit. He takes the whole Soul into this union. Eucharist!

Part of your mind is a talking computer. You are not this. You can talk to this part of yourself and reprogram the computer.

What is happening, subject-to-subject, is the greatest mystery. I and Thou become We, which is more than I *plus* Thou. This can be experienced and to some extent described, but never defined.

They are, every one of them, your brothers and Sisters, made of exactly the same "stuff" that you are. They are, most of them, caught up in desire, delusion, and ignorance, just like you once were. Love them for who they are, not for who they "think" they are.

Christ himself speaks through the intuitive function. His Word elicits an immediate consensual response from the other faculties. When Christ speaks—even of doing a hard thing—his words bring peace. Other "voices" leave the mind disturbed.

The leaders of the world religions sit on a treasure of gold (their mystical traditions), tossing out Mardi Gras tokens to the people.

Drop your attachments and follow your heart. Drop dissipating thoughts and behaviors, and the healthy "you" will emerge most naturally and beautifully. Quit making yourself sick, and you shall be well. How simple it is! How difficult!

SUGGESTED READING

Alcoholics Anonymous. *Twelve Steps and Twelve Traditions.* New York: Alcoholics Anonymous World Services, Inc., 1952.

Arraj, James. *The Inner Nature of Faith: A Mysterious Knowledge Coming Through the Heart.* Chiloquin, OR: Inner Growth Books, 1988.

de Mello, Anthony, S.J. *Awareness: A De Mello Spirituality Conference in His Own Words.* New York: Doubleday, 1990.

Greene, Thomas. *When the Well Runs Dry: Prayer Beyond the Beginnings.* Notre Dame, IN: Ave Maria Press, 1979.

Groeschel, Benedict J. *Spiritual Passages: For Those Who Seek.* New York: Crossroad, 1988.

Johnston, William. *Being in Love: The Practice of Christian Prayer.* San Francisco: Harper and Row, 1995.

_____. *Mystical Theology: The Science of Love.* San Francisco: Harper and Row, 1995.

Keating, Thomas. *Open Mind, Open Heart: The Contemplative Dimension of the Gospel.* Rockport, MA: Element Books, 1991.

_____. *Invitation to Love.* Rockport, MA: Element Books, 1992.

Lange, Joseph and Anthony Cushing. *Friendship With Jesus.* Pecos, NM: Dove Publications, 1974.

May, Gerald. *Will and Spirit: A Contemplative Psychology.* San Francisco: Harper and Row, 1982.

_____. *Addiction and Grace: Love and Spirituality in the Healing of Addictions.* San Francisco: Harper and Row, 1988.

McCormick, Patrick, C.M. *Sin As Addiction.* Mahwah, NJ: Paulist Press, 1989.

Royo, Antonio, O.P., and Jordan Aumann, O.P. *The Theology of Christian Perfection.* Dubuque, IA: The Priory Press, 1962.

Schaef, Anne Wilson. *When Society Becomes an Addict.* San Francisco: Harper and Row, 1987.

Saint Teresa of Avila. *The Interior Castle.* New York: Doubleday, 1972.

Tugwell, Simon, O.P. *Ways of Imperfection.* Springfield, IL: Templegate, 1985.

Westley, Dick. *Theology of Presence: The Search for Meaning in the American Catholic Experience.* Mystic, CT: Twenty-third Publications, 1989.

Woods, Richard. *Christian Spirituality.* Chicago: Thomas More Press, 1989.